HOW
DEMOCRATIC
IS
THE
UNITED STATES?

BY MICHAEL KRONENWETTER

DEMOCRACY IN ACTION

FRANKLIN WATTS
NEW YORK/CHICAGO/LONDON/TORONTO/SYDNEY

Library of Congress Cataloging-in-Publication Data

Kronenwetter, Michael.
How democratic is the United States? / by Michael Kronenwetter.
p.   cm.—(Democracy in action)
Includes bibliographical references and index.
ISBN 0-531-11155-5
1. United States—Politics and government.   2. Democracy—United
States.   [1. United States—Politics and government.
2. Democracy.]   I. Title.   II. Series: Democracy in action
(Franklin Watts, Inc.)
JK271.K76   1994   94-13718   CIP   AC
324.6′3′0973—dc20

CONTENTS

FOREWORD

"I think we've lost our country," mourned a recent caller to a national television program. "The government is corrupt."[1]

Political corruption is the misuse or abuse of power, either by individual officials or by the government itself. The caller was reflecting a growing sense that our government is not doing its job—that it no longer truly represents the people of the United States and their interests.

"There's been a ton of evidence for the last thirty or forty years, that Americans are . . . cynical about government," says Professor Jack Johnanes of Marquette University.[2] A 1992 poll found that 56 percent of the people agreed with the statement that the "economic and political systems in [the United States] are stacked against people like me."[3] A more recent poll found that over 85 percent of the American public doesn't even trust the government to do what's right most of the time.[4]

This negative attitude toward the government may be growing, but it is nothing new. Americans have never trusted their government. Most of them have never liked it very much, either. Why should they? The United States was born in a revolution against government, and a deep suspicion of government has run under the surface of American political life ever since.

In a way, that suspicion is built into the American political system. The Founding Fathers wanted to be sure that the government they established would be firmly under the control of the people of the country, not the other way around. Democratic procedures were installed to make it hard for the new government to bully and oppress the people the way the British king had done.

During more than two centuries of United States history, politicians have come and gone. Some have been extremely popular for a while—but only with a part of the population. Even the most popular American presidents had hordes of opponents and detractors. In fact, the leaders who inspired the most passionate support were usually the ones who also aroused the most bitter opposition. Andrew Jackson, Abraham Lincoln, Franklin Roosevelt, and Ronald Reagan were all among the best-loved American presidents, but they were also among the most despised.

By the early 1990s, the traditional American distrust of government power had become a widespread hostility toward the government itself—combined with a lack of respect for the people who ran it. Congress's reputation had already been badly damaged by a series of scandals in the late 1980s. When President George Bush ran for re-election in 1992, he received less than 40 percent of the vote—one of the worst beatings ever for an incumbent president. Even the winner, Bill Clinton, got only 43 percent of the vote, which was nearly as low as any victorious president has ever received. What's more, Clinton's standing in the public opinion polls began to drop dramatically almost as soon as he was in office.

Even the United States Supreme Court did not escape the public's distaste. Senate hearings involving a nominee to the Court, Clarence Thomas, produced a national scandal when Anita Hill charged him with making unwanted sexual advances to her years before. Although

Thomas hotly denied the charges, both he and the Court were stained.

Worse than any of this was a widespread sense that the federal government was not really accomplishing anything. That it was unable, or unwilling, to govern the country. Eighty-one percent of the people asked in a 1992 poll believed that the country was on the wrong track.[5] More and more people expressed anger and despair over their government. A 1992 presidential candidate, Jerry Brown, spoke of "a deep and growing disconnection" between the people and the government.[6]

How can this be? The United States prides itself on being the world's leading democracy. The people of the United States have had more say in our government, over a longer time, than the people of any other nation on earth. So how can we feel excluded? How can we be so dissatisfied? Have we really lost our country? Has our democratic system really been taken over by corrupt and hostile forces?

In this book we will explore the American political system and some of the criticisms often directed at it. We will ask how democratic it actually is and how it might be made more so. The first step in this exploration is to find out what a democracy is and what it is meant to do.

THE
PEOPLE RULE

The word *democracy* means "rule by the people." In modern political terms it means a form of government in which the final authority rests with the ordinary citizens of the country. The people decide who should serve in the government and what the government should do.

Democracy is not a new idea. The Greek philosophers Plato and Aristotle wrote about democracy 2,500 years ago. There were democratic forms of government, of sorts, in the city-states of ancient Greece and Rome, and many Indian tribes in North America were governed even more democratically.

During most of the past two thousand years, however, the governments of most countries were monarchies of one kind or another. Instead of being ruled by the people, they were ruled by kings or queens, often with the help of a small class of powerful nobles. The modern movement toward democracy began in England in the middle of the seventeenth century. Within 150 years, it had spread thoughout Europe. Although the European nations kept their monarchs, they put more and more of the real power in the hands of elected officials chosen to represent the people.

Late in the eighteenth century, the United States

became the first major nation to get rid of its monarch—
the British king—altogether. France did the same a few
years later. Today the few monarchs who remain in the
Western world are virtually powerless.

Modern democracy was a response to what the people saw as the tyranny of government. It is built on distrust
of government and on a belief in the rights of individual
people. It has been said that it's the evil in man that makes
democracy necessary, and man's belief in justice that
makes democracy possible.[1]

———— THE SIGNS OF DEMOCRACY ————

There are many forms of democratic government. Some
are more successful, and more fundamentally democratic,
than others. But they all share certain ideals and attributes
that are recognized as necessary to democracy.

FREEDOM
"Liberty," declared Aristotle, "is the basis of a democratic state."[2] The right of people to live free of domination by others is the most fundmental goal of democracy.
What good would it be for the people to rule a nation if
they could not rule their own lives and govern their own
actions?

MAJORITY RULE
Individuals should be free to make their own decisions.
But if each individual has the right to govern himself or
herself, then no one has the right to govern others. And yet
nations have to be governed. Decisions have to be made—
decisions that affect not just individuals but the whole
society. In such cases, Aristotle declared, "the majority
must be supreme."[3] In effect, "the will of the people"
means the will of *the majority* of the people.

Individuals and groups within any society have different ideas and interests. Some might think that the government should provide health insurance to all citizens. Others may believe that the government has no business providing health insurance to anyone. Some will think that the country should destroy all its nuclear weapons. Others will think that it should build more of them. There may be compromises along the way, but one side or the other will eventually win the argument. Either the government will provide health insurance or it won't. Nuclear weapons will be destroyed or they won't.

In most democratic systems, such questions are finally put to a vote, either by the people themselves or by their elected representatives. In the end, the side with the most votes will have its way.

PROTECTION OF THE RIGHTS OF MINORITIES

The basic problem for any democracy is how to balance the conflict between individual liberty and majority rule. The will of the majority becomes the law, but that law must protect the rights of everyone, not just those of the majority. "[T]hough the will of the majority is in all cases to prevail, that will to be rightful must be reasonable," Thomas Jefferson declared. "[T]he minority possess their equal rights, which equal law must protect." This, said Jefferson, is a "sacred principle" of democracy.[4]

Every citizen in a democracy has the same basic rights as every other citizen, whether that person is in the majority or not. Each one holds those rights as an individual, not as a member of some group. In the American system those rights are protected by the U.S. Constitution.

The Constitution contains the fundamental law of the land. No state or federal law can overrule it and take away a constitutional right from any citizen. No law that tries to do so is really legal. The Constitution itself is a very difficult document to change. Reducing or eliminating a constitutional right would require the approval of two-thirds of both houses of Congress, and of the legislatures of three-quarters of the states.

ELECTIONS

Governments, proclaimed Thomas Jefferson in the Declaration of Independence, derive "their just powers from the consent of the governed." In a modern democracy this consent is primarily expressed through elections in which the voters choose people to serve in the government.

Although we tend to take elections for granted, they are not the only possible way to choose leaders in a democracy. Aristotle suggested that leaders might be picked by lot: since no citizen had a right to rule over the others, it was only fair that everyone have a chance to govern. In practice, however, most democratic countries have decided that it is better for people to have a choice of who should lead them.

Elected officials serve for limited periods of time. In the United States, members of Congress serve for two years, presidents for four, and senators for six. This is because "the consent of the governed" has to be ongoing. The people must have a chance to change their minds and choose new representatives if the current ones fail to live up to expectations, or even if the citizens simply get tired of them.

—— THE PURPOSE OF DEMOCRACY ——

Majority rule is not necessarily designed to produce the most efficient, or the most practical, decisions for the country. If that were its main goal, then democracy would be a poor form of government. There are certainly better ways to reach practical decisions than to rely on the opinion of the majority.

Despite their commitment to democracy, even many of the nation's founders distrusted the common sense of the majority. "The people are turbulent and changing," declared Alexander Hamilton. "[T]hey seldom judge or determine right."[5]

There is no doubt that some people have better judgment than others and know more about specific issues than the majority of people do. Just as clearly, some people are more concerned with the well-being of society as a whole, while others are more concerned with their own self-interest. It may well be that a single intelligent, well-informed, and public-spirited person would make more sensible decisions than the masses of people.

Why, then, should there be majority rule at all? The answer has more to do with liberty and fairness than with wisdom. Majority rule is based on the belief that every person has a *right* to a say in the decisions that govern his or her life. That right is not based on the intelligence or nobility of the individual. It is not based on any personal quality at all. It is a fundamental human right, which everyone has by virtue of being human.

Although we all have the right to make our own decisions, we cannot, acting alone, make decisions for everyone else. For one thing, we have no right to do so. For another, each of us would make different decisions. The result would be chaos. The democratic answer is to give each individual a voice in the decision. The more nearly equal that voice, the more democratic the political system.

"A REPUBLIC, SIR, IF YOU CAN KEEP IT!"

The United States government was conceived in secret. The fifty-five delegates to the Constitutional Convention in Philadelphia met behind closed doors. It is said that when the convention was over, one eager citizen rushed up to Benjamin Franklin and asked what kind of government the country was to have.

"A republic, sir," Franklin replied, "if you can keep it!"

Franklin meant that the government would be a representative democracy. James Madison, who is called "the father of the Constitution," defined a republican government as one "which derives all its powers directly or indirectly from the great body of the people." He went on to emphasize that "[i]t is essential to such a government that it be derived from the great body of the society, not from . . . a favored class of it."[1] In the new American republic, "the great body of the people" would rule indirectly, through elected representatives.

——— REPRESENTATIVE DEMOCRACY ———

The earliest forms of democratic government were direct democracies. The citizens of an ancient Greek city-state would meet in the town center to decide important issues. The members of North American tribes gathered in a longhouse or around a campfire to elect their chief.

Modern democracies, starting with the one formed in Philadelphia in 1787, are not like that. Instead of all citizens meeting together to make important decisions, they elect individuals to make decisions for them.

Representative democracies try to achieve the same goal as direct democracies—to provide ordinary citizens with an effective voice in the decisions that affect their lives. But that voice is filtered through the intelligence and judgment of the individuals chosen to govern in the people's name.

The founders had several reasons for rejecting the idea of a direct democracy. For one thing, there were simply too many people in the new country, and too much space, for a direct democracy to work. The ancient democracies could function because the number of citizens was limited. Most American Indian tribes were small, and lived and traveled together. In ancient Greece, citizenship was restricted to a relatively small number of people. Most city-states had only a few thousand residents, and most of them were either women or slaves, neither of whom could participate in government.

A few hundred people can meet, debate, and then reach a decision. But tens of thousands—much less millions—cannot. It is impossible for the residents of an entire state or nation to gather together. Even if they could all travel to one place, they could never crowd into even the largest meeting hall, nor could they hear each other out in argument.

But even if a direct democracy had been possible, the founders probably would have rejected it. They were responsible, educated men, and they thought that society should be governed by men like themselves. Most of them believed in democratic principles like freedom and individual rights, but they still feared what one of them called "the turbulence and follies" of the masses of the people.[2]

The people could turn into a mob. The most thoughtful founders were just as frightened of the tyranny of the majority as they were of the tyranny of any monarch. They understood that unbridled power was dangerous, whether that power was in the hands of a single person or in the hands of the mob. The concentration of power in *any* hands, wrote Madison, is "precisely the definition of despotic government."[3]

The writers of the Constitution wanted the government to respond to the will of men like themselves—men who owned property and had some stake in the prosperity and stability of the community. (They did not even consider giving women the vote, to say nothing of the right to serve in the government.)

There was another practical consideration, too. Most people of common sense had better things to do with their time and energies than operate the government. They had work to do: farmland to till, plantations to run, or other business to attend to. They could not be expected to inform themselves in detail about every matter of national concern, much less to run the day-to-day affairs of government. Representatives would have to be chosen to do these things for them.

The founders wanted to be sure these representatives would have the wisdom and experience to make good judgments, and the practical ability to run a government. Just as importantly, they wanted men who would put the republic's well-being before their own. They did not want the government to fall into the hands of men ruled by what Hamilton described as the "avarice, ambition, and interest which govern most people."[4] In short, they wanted men like George Washington, whom they elected to be chairman of the Convention.

For all these reasons, then, the founders devised a whole new system of government. That system was designed to be more democratic than any other in the world, but it was also designed to guard against *too much* democracy. Of the three branches of government, only one—the House of Representatives—would be elected directly by the people. Senators would be chosen by the legislatures of their states, and the president would be picked by the vote of a "Number of Electors." Each state would "appoint" its own electors "in such manner as the Legislature thereof may direct."

The founders worried that if the choice of presidents and senators was left entirely to popular acclaim, the people would pick rabble-rousers to lead them: irresponsible firebrands who could stir up a crowd but couldn't run a government. Or who, if they could, would use the power of government to achieve their own selfish ends, not the good of society as a whole.

The government established by the Constitutional Convention, including the methods of electing senators and presidents, would be changed in later years. But it is important to realize that it was originally designed not only to keep the government under the people's control but to keep the people under control as well.

_____ CHECKS AND BALANCES _____

As everyone knows, the government of the United States has three main branches: the legislative, the executive, and the judicial. Generally put, the legislative branch makes the laws by which the government operates; the judicial branch interprets those laws, including the Constitution; while the executive branch carries out the laws and runs the operations of the government, including the military.

While each branch has its own job to do, each also

acts as a kind of brake on the others. Congress may pass laws, but it needs the executive branch to enforce them. The courts may overrule the Congress and declare a law unconstitutional, but the Congress can, with help from the people, change the Constitution. And so on.

In addition, the power of the federal government is further checked by the fact that the state governments have their own rights and powers. For the most part, however, the federal government dominates, and it is primarily the federal government we are concerned with here.

The fact that no branch is free to do much entirely on its own is an important safeguard of the rights and liberties of the people. This helps to prevent any branch from becoming tyrannical. But this complex system can also make it hard to get things done.

___ COMPROMISE AND ACCEPTANCE ___

The United States was born in compromise. It had to be. The men who founded it represented thirteen very different states with different governments, different societies, and different economic interests. As individuals, they had opposing ideas about what the new system should be.

Some, like Alexander Hamilton, wanted a strong national government that would forge thirteen separate states into a single strong nation and build a prosperous economy for it. Others, like William Paterson of New Jersey, wanted to make sure the state governments retained their independence. Several delegates from northern states hoped to see slavery abolished, while many from the South hoped to see the practice protected by the new Constitution. Some, like James Madison, wanted representatives to the new government elected directly by the people. Others, like Paterson, wanted them to be chosen by the state legislatures. And so on.

The compromise that resulted from these conflicts gave birth to the U.S. political system, and has remained a model for democratic government ever since.

The key to the effectiveness of any democratic system is the way it handles the competing interests and opinions of its citizens. Different people want and expect different things from the government. The government has to decide which of those desires and expectations to satisfy and which to reject. In a democracy it is important that the people as a whole believe that these decisions have been made fairly. Even those whose interests are ignored or damaged have to accept the decisions and the process that made them.

In theory there are two ways to settle the disputes that are bound to arise in any democracy. In the first, the issue is argued out and then resolved one way or another. One side wins, and the other side loses. In the second way of settling disputes, a compromise is worked out in which each side gets a part of what it wants, but no side is fully satisfied. In the United States, most politicians favor the second alternative. "Honorable compromise," President Bill Clinton once said, "is what democracy is all about."[5] To reach a compromise, it is usually necessary for all sides to give up part of what they want to the others.

Those who, like Clinton, believe in compromise usually reject radical proposals: programs and policies in which one side gets exactly what it wants, while the other loses out. When put into effect, they argue, such proposals lead to bitterness, resentment, and alienation. Those who lose out feel betrayed and battered by the political system, and they lose confidence in it.

Ultimately this is dangerous for a democracy. For when people lose faith in the system, they often turn to nondemocratic forms of government. In a speech to the Constitutional Convention, Benjamin Franklin predicted that the republic would only survive until "the people shall become so corrupted as to need despotic government, being incapable of any other."[6]

When radical proposals are made, the compromisers search for ways to change them so they become more acceptable to all sides. This is, in fact, what usually happens in the U.S. Congress, where compromises are made before almost any proposal is enacted into law.

Not everyone believes that compromise is an ideal solution. Some argue that there is no conflict between democracy and radical change. If the majority of the people want some fundamental change in economic or social policy, they should get it. The losers in the conflict may be angry and bitter, but there is no reason for them to reject democracy. Just the opposite. After all, the radical change came about through democratic means. And what has been changed can be changed again—at least so long as the democratic process remains in place.

The key to making democracy work is the willingness of people to accept the results reached through the democratic process. This means that those who lose out in a democratic decision, however radical, need to accept that decision. But it also means that those who win must accept the possibility that the decision could be reversed in the future. The potential for change is a fundamental element of democracy. "The basis of our political system," said George Washington, "is the right of the people to make and to alter their constitutions of government."[7]

Franklin's response to the man who asked him about the form of the new government was as much a warning as an explanation. He assumed, along with most other Americans of that time, that a republic was a fragile thing. Kings and queens could rule by decree. But a republic would need the acceptance and cooperation of the people. Specific programs might be opposed by large numbers of people, but the system must assure all of them that their interests have been taken into account. They must never become so hopeless or so impatient that they turn to despotic government.

Franklin knew that the success of the American republic would depend on the strength, courage, determination, and most of all the public-spiritedness of its citizens. If the republican government was to survive, the people would have to put aside some of their selfish interests and accept and cooperate with one another.

TWEEDLEDUM AND TWEEDLEDEE— OR IS IT THE OTHER WAY AROUND?

In his farewell address as president, George Washington warned the country against political factions—or parties. If they were allowed to develop, he warned, they would destroy the democratic process. Although they might sometimes *seem* to do the people's will, in the long run they would "put in the place of the delegated will of the nation the will of a party." They would allow "cunning, ambitious, and unprincipled men . . . to usurp the power of the people" and destroy the very democracy that had "lifted them to unjust domination."[1]

Washington was worried that if the people who ran the government split into factions, they would quarrel for power among themselves instead of concentrating on finding the best solutions to the country's problems. Yet parties were already forming when Washington spoke; and the two centuries that have passed since seem to prove that parties are an inevitable offshoot of democracy. Political parties exist in every country with a democratic form of government.

This is not surprising. Different people and groups have different, and often conflicting, needs and desires. It is only natural for those with common purposes to unite to promote them and to oppose those whose goals are contrary to theirs.

THE REPUBLICANS AND THE DEMOCRATS

For more than a century, political life has been dominated by just two parties: the Republicans and the Democrats. At different times, one party or the other has had the upper hand. The Republicans, for example, were dominant in the 1920s, the Democrats in the 1930s. For the past half century, however, the two parties have tended to share power between them.

For most of that time, Democrats have held a majority in both houses of Congress while the presidency has changed hands between the parties. Despite the Democratic domination of the legislative branch, Republicans have won the presidency in five out of the last seven elections.

The Democrats and Republicans have made themselves essential to the way the American political system operates. It is the parties that choose the nominees for major political office in this country. Every president since 1852 was nominated by one of the two parties, as was every current member of the Senate and all but one current member of the House of Representatives.

PARTISANSHIP VERSUS BIPARTISANSHIP

George Washington was worried that partisanship—the rivalry between the two parties—would divide the government and make cooperation for the public good impossible. And yet the two major parties have often been surprisingly bipartisan. They frequently work together to accomplish national goals. During the Second World

War, for example, the parties united to promote the war effort.

A certain amount of cooperation usually takes place even when the official party organizations take strongly opposed positions. Some members of each party typically cooperate with the majority of the other party to accomplish shared goals. At times when neither party controls the entire government, this kind of cooperation is vital in order to get anything done.

Even when one party seems to control both the legislative branch and executive branch of government, some bipartisan cooperation is often necessary. That is because not all members of either party can be counted on to support their party's position on every issue. Some moderate Republicans, who are more liberal than most of their Republican colleagues, will join with the Democrats on particular issues. Some moderate Democrats, more conservative than most of their colleagues, will join with the Republicans.

As a result, only minor measures are typically passed or voted down on straight party-line votes, with every member of Congress voting with his or her party. Most major bills are the products of compromise. Few important proposals are passed without some changes made to win the support of members of the other party.

One exception to this was the budget proposed by President Clinton in 1993, a proposal that the Republicans in both the House and the Senate united to oppose at every step. Every Republican member of the House and Senate budget committees voted against every aspect of the president's plan in key votes. Refusing to compromise, or even to negotiate, they left the Democrats to work out a budget among themselves. When the budget finally came to the floor of the House and the Senate, the Republicans kept up their united front and voted solidly against it.

This total noncooperation was unusual on such important legislation. It was the first time in almost fifty years that a major economic bill had failed to receive the vote of even one member of the opposing party.

Each side blamed the other for the failure to cooperate. The Democrats charged that the Republicans had deliberately chosen to sit on the sidelines and snipe at the Democrats rather than help develop a budget that would be good for the country. The Republicans, on the other hand, charged that the Democrats had refused to negotiate with them.

But it wasn't just the budget that the Republicans refused to cooperate on. They balked at almost every measure proposed by the Clinton administration in the spring and summer of 1993, even when it meant reversing the stand they had taken when a Republican was president. The Republican minority leader in the Senate, Bob Dole, led a filibuster to delay the president's plan to provide college aid for young people in return for two years of national service. Meanwhile, the House Republicans even did their best, with the help of some rebellious Democrats, to hold up a bill giving disaster relief to victims of the great Midwest flood of 1993. They complained that the bill provided no specific way to pay for the relief and that it contained a good many measures that had nothing to do with the flood.

Through all this, the Republicans insisted that they were acting on principle. They disagreed with the president's policies, they said, and felt bound to oppose them. But the Democrats had a different explanation for the Republicans' refusal to cooperate: partisanship. The Republicans, the Democrats insisted, were acting for the good of their party, not that of the country.

"They don't want this president to have a record of achievement," declared Senator Barbara Boxer of

California.[2] Representative Sander Levin, a Democrat from Michigan, complained on the floor of the House that the Republicans had become nothing but "a band of attack dogs." The public, he said, "expects better of the loyal opposition."[3] "It doesn't bode well for the country," lamented Democratic senator Harry Reid of Nevada.[4] Vice President Al Gore publicly complained that the Republican senators' effort to scuttle the administration's programs was "breathtakingly cynical" and ignored the national interest.[5]

Even so, the noncooperation stopped short of total obstruction. There was no Republican filibuster against the budget bill that might have really scuttled it; the Republican resistance to flood relief was only temporary; and a compromise was ultimately reached on the national service–student aid bill. Even in the bitter summer of 1993, then, both sides recognized that the country has to be governed despite partisan differences. At some point there has to be enough cooperation between the political factions to see to it that the government continues to function.

⎯ A DIME'S WORTH OF DIFFERENCE? ⎯

Ironically, the lack of negotiation and compromise between the parties didn't seem to make much difference to the final budget plan itself. Individual Democratic senators and congresspersons had their own axes to grind, and they chopped away at various sections of the president's plan in much the same way the Republicans might have done. In the end, the budget that passed by one vote in the Democrat-dominated House was not the one originally proposed by President Clinton. Overall, the budget produced by the Democratic Congress did not raise taxes nearly as much as the Democratic president had called for, and spent somewhat less than he had requested. In fact, it was not so different than it might have been if the Democrats and Republicans had worked it out between them.

The 1993 budget demonstrates one of the major complaints some critics have of the way the two major parties operate, and the control they exercise over national political life. The public arguing between them was fierce and often angry. Great issues were involved, and enormous interests were at stake. Both sides declared that they were fighting for important principles. The majority of Democrats voted one way; all the Republicans voted the other way. On the surface, it seemed a fierce battle between two different political philosophies. And yet many observers felt that it was a sham struggle in which both sides were more interested in scoring political points than in solving the country's economic problems.

At bottom, the budget battle was more a struggle over the future of President Clinton than over the future of the country. The Republicans refused to cooperate in shaping what they would have considered a better bill precisely because they wanted to see the Democratic president fail. Many Democrats disliked the bill but voted for it because they feared that if it didn't pass, Clinton would become a failed president. The key vote belonged to Senator Robert Kerrey of Nebraska, a Democrat, who declared on the Senate floor that he was voting for it because he was not prepared to see the president destroyed.

Both parties agreed that the economy was suffocating under a huge national debt that had already reached 4 trillion dollars and was climbing out of sight. Yet neither party actually put forward a program designed to reduce, much less to eliminate, that debt. Instead, they argued mostly over relatively insignificant details of proposals that were not very different from each other in the first place—proposals critics insisted wouldn't do much to reduce the national debt in any case.

"This has become a battle between the Republicans

and the Democrats," complained independent presidential candidate H. Ross Perot. "A lot of good ideas aren't even being considered."[6]

Sooner or later almost all American political controversies do become battles between the Republicans and the Democrats. And, as Perot and other critics on both the Right and the Left complain, good ideas are often ignored while the two parties fight over votes instead of principles.

—————— SCRAMBLING FOR THE ——————
POLITICAL CENTER

The critics charge that the two main parties have little or no ideology—that is, no real political beliefs—of their own. They have become little more than campaign organizations, helping candidates who go by the label "Democrat" or "Republican" get elected and reelected. The trouble is that the labels are almost meaningless. "There isn't a dime's worth of difference between them," declared independent presidential candidate George Wallace in 1968.[7]

Wallace was an Alabama conservative and segregationist who was angered by what he saw as the federal government's interference in his state's right to set its own social policies. But his criticism of the two major parties is echoed by critics from all over the political spectrum. All complain that the parties are far too similar to reflect the true range of views of the American people.

In fact, there are some significant differences in the way the two parties view society and government, and the relationship between them. In general, the Democrats favor more government involvement in the economy than do the Republicans. They also tend to be more liberal on social issues than the Republicans, to favor more government programs to help the poor and disadvantaged, and to be more willing to spend money on such programs. The Republicans, on the other hand, are generally more concerned with property rights and the rights of businesses than the Democrats are. And so on.

Even so, the Democrats and Republicans do represent a relatively narrow range of political beliefs and approaches, compared to parties in most other democratic countries. The differences between them tend to be largely in emphasis and approach rather than in fundamental principles. Both parties try to occupy the political center—that is, they take positions that they believe most Americans will agree with. They try hard to avoid supporting measures that are controversial enough to turn off potential voters.

As a result, they argue about things like how much to cut spending on nuclear weapons rather than whether to eliminate nuclear weapons altogether. How much the government should regulate industry-produced pollution instead of whether the government should protect the environment at all. Whatever fundamental ideology, or political beliefs, they have, they seem to share in common.

For example, both parties favor:

The current American political system. Neither party proposes any change in the basic structure of the American government as established by the Constitution.

Capitalism. Both parties believe in private property and the free enterprise economic system. Each supports measures designed to encourage American business, although they frequently disagree about which measures are most likely to succeed. At the same time, both parties favor some governmental regulation of business, particularly where the public health and safety are concerned. Their disagreements center on what limits should be set on that regulation.

A strong military. Although they often disagree about levels of troop strength, and the need for particular new weapons systems, both parties favor keeping the United States the most powerful military nation in the world.

On the other hand, neither party favors:

Unilateral nuclear disarmament. At least as long as other countries have the ability to produce nuclear weapons, both parties believe the United States should continue to maintain and improve its own nuclear capacity. Despite the end of the Cold War, neither party wants the United States to dismantle its nuclear stockpile.

Government ownership of industry. Neither party wants to see the government take over vital industries like steel, transportation, and weapons manufacturing.

Abolishing the federal income tax. Although the Republicans traditionally favor lower income tax rates than the Democrats, even they do not call for abandoning the income tax altogether.

In essence, the two main parties are fighting over the center of the American political spectrum. They know that that's where most votes are. As a result, neither party is eager, or even willing, to propose radically new solutions to the nation's problems.

—————— TWO JAWS OF A VISE ——————

Some Americans do favor such things as unilateral nuclear disarmament, government ownership of key industries, and abolishing the income tax. Many others might be willing to consider other radical approaches to stubborn problems that haven't been solved by the traditional measures favored by the two main parties. But the fact that both parties reject such controversial proposals effectively kills any chance for them to be adopted by the

American government—or even seriously considered by the American people.

For the most part, the two parties set the boundaries of serious political debate. They are like the two jaws of a vise that squeeze the political debate between them. Unless one or the other decides that an idea is worth consideration, it is unlikely to be adopted, either by the government or by the public.

Supporters of the two-party system argue that the parties perform a valuable service as gatekeepers. The government is busy enough. Officeholders cannot afford to spend time considering every new political idea that someone wants to suggest. The parties weed out impractical and crackpot ideas and allow serious politicians to concentrate on the middle-of-the-road measures most Americans would consider realistic.

Even critics would agree that there has to be some limit on the number of political measures seriously debated at the national level. But they complain that the range of ideas represented by the two parties is much too narrow. Both parties have been around for a long time now, and they are set in their ways. Critics like Ross Perot complain that the two parties have a stranglehold on American political debate, and choke off any idea that doesn't fit comfortably within the political center.

The fact that new ideas are not currently supported by either party doesn't mean that they are not worthwhile. Once the public examines some of these ideas, they might become more popular. In time, a majority of the people might even come to support them. But this is not likely to happen as long as neither party takes them up. Since neither party has any interest in disarming unilaterally or abolishing the income tax, for example, people who do will have little chance to air their case before the nation.

The problem for the democratic process is not that such measures can't be passed into law at the moment; there is nothing undemocratic about that, since they are not favored by most Americans. The problem is that ideas like these cannot even be seriously debated at the national level.

——— HOW THE PARTIES CONTROL ——— THE DEBATE

What do the critics mean when thay complain that the major parties control the political debate? How can they control it? After all, this is a democratic country, with freedom of speech and the press. Anyone can say anything he or she wants to say.

It's true that the parties don't prevent citizens from expressing their ideas. But, say the critics, the parties do keep those ideas from having much effect on the actual government of the United States. They are able to do this because they dominate all levels of government.

Every president in modern times has been either a Republican or a Democrat. Only one current governor, Lowell Weicker, of Connecticut, is an independent, and even he used to be a Republican. Only one of the 535 current members of the House and Senate—Representative Bernard Sanders of Vermont—is neither a Democrat nor a Republican. In addition, members of the two parties control every state legislature in the country. This means that no bill can pass anywhere that isn't supported by at least one of the two major parties.

What's more, the national media rely on spokespeople for the parties as their main source of political information. Outsiders are rarely taken seriously and therefore rarely get a chance to express their ideas in the national press or on network and cable television. Ross Perot was an important exception to this rule in 1992, but Perot was a billionaire who was able to bypass the parties because of his money. It is unlikely that the national media would have taken him seriously, and therefore given him space and time to reach the public, without it.

THE SPECIAL INTERESTS

"Our democratic system has been the object of a hostile takeover," announced presidential candidate Jerry Brown in 1992. "Politics have been debased, and citizens have been excluded from genuinely participating in the economic and political life of their community."[1]

If the citizens have been excluded, who is in control? According to Brown and other critics, the answer is the special interests.

___ WHO ARE THE SPECIAL INTERESTS? ___

Who are the special interests?
We are.

Most people think of a special interest as something distant and sinister. Something that involves *other* people. Something they have no part in themselves. In reality, however, virtually every American is represented by some special interest.

Society is more than a collection of individuals. It is made up of many different elements: groups of people united by common interests and concerns. Each of us belongs to many of these groups. We are male or female.

We are young, or middle-aged, or old. We are students, workers, doctors, homemakers, or whatever.

Each of these categories is a special interest—that is, its members have particular worries, desires, and goals that are different, to some extent, from the concerns of society in general. The elderly, for example, are especially concerned with the need for affordable long-term health care. Parents, students, and teachers are especially concerned with keeping the educational system up to date. And so on.

There are all kinds of special interests in the United States today. Big business is a special interest, but so is small business. Conservative Christians are a special interest. Gays and lesbians are a special interest. Lawyers are a special interest. So are farmers; African Americans, Asian Americans, and other ethnic groups; environmentalists, union members, gun owners, children, people on welfare, and so on.

Each of these broad special interests contains smaller special interests. Big business is a special interest, and yet chemical companies, automobile manufacturers, tobacco companies, steel producers, and drug companies each have needs and worries that are not shared by the others, each of which seeks its own advantages. All farmers share certain goals. They want to keep property taxes on farmlands as low as possible, for example. But different kinds of farmers also have different concerns. Dairy farmers are concerned with things like milk prices, which grain farmers have no interest in. Sometimes different groups of farmers are in direct conflict. Owners of small family farms, for example, often oppose measures that benefit the operators of the huge corporate farms that threaten to drive them out of business.

Special interests have always played a vital role in American history. Agricultural interests dominated the founding of the United States. The railroads and the developing manufacturing industries were enormously powerful in Washington during the nineteenth century, shaping policy as the nation spread across the continent. Organized labor helped shape the policies of the New Deal and the Fair Deal. The pressure and lobbying of the civil rights movement of the 1950s and 1960s brought about an end to legal racial segregation.

There are literally thousands of special interests in the United States today. For good or bad, they play important parts in the American political process. Partly this is because their common concerns often cause members of special interests to vote as a bloc. But it is also because many special interests are represented by *special interest groups,* organizations that work to promote the goals of the interest they represent.

Some of these groups are very small. Others are large and immensely powerful. The strong organizations include the National Rifle Association (NRA), which promotes the cause of gun manufacturers and owners; the American Medical Association (AMA), which is made up largely of physicians; and the American Association of Retired People (AARP), which works to benefit older Americans. Groups like these have enormous influence on government.

They exert this influence in several ways. They run public relations campaigns to persuade the public to take their side. They organize voters to elect candidates who support the causes they believe in and to oppose candidates who do not. And they approach politicians and other government officials directly through lobbyists.

THE ROLE OF LOBBYISTS

Every citizen has a right to lobby—that is, to attempt to influence government policy and actions. That right is central to the whole idea of democracy. In the United

States it is a constitutional right guaranteed by the First Amendment, which protects freedom of speech and "the right of the people . . . to petition the Government for a redress of grievances."

Some "grass roots" lobbyists are, in fact, ordinary citizens, volunteers acting to promote the interests of groups to which they belong. Others, however, are professionals: paid employees of special interest groups, hired to influence the government on their behalf.

Washington, D.C., is filled with lobbying firms that sell their services to almost anyone who is able to pay. They are staffed by skilled and knowledgeable people who know, or claim to know, how to influence goverment policy for their clients. They include public relations people, business executives, and accountants as well as ex-politicians and former government employees.

Federal law requires people who spend at least 50 percent of their professional time dealing directly with congresspeople on behalf of clients to register with the government. Roughly six thousand lobbyists have done so, according to Jim Thurber, professor of Public Affairs at American University.[2] Thurber and other observers believe that this is only a fraction of the actual number of professional lobbyists in Washington, however. Most of the rest lobby part-time, or spend most of their time preparing approaches, fund-raising, or dealing with non-congressional government officials.

Lobbyists perform a number of functions. Among others, they plead their clients' cases to government officials. In doing so, they provide a great deal of information to congresspeople about issues related to bills coming up before the House and Senate. The information presented by some lobbyists is extremely one-sided, and needs to be taken with a grain of salt. Other lobbyists have a reputation for providing full and accurate information, which the elected officials are grateful to get. It often includes vital facts and figures that overworked congressional staff members would never come up with on their own.

Lobbyists supply information to the press as well. In fact, much of what the press reports about some issues is what the lobbyists have told them. The lobbyists like to provide information to the press because this helps them to manipulate the way television, newspapers, and the other media present the issues that affect their clients. Eventually public opinion, which the lobbyists help mold, will help the lobbyists persuade the politicians to do what their clients want done.

HIRED GUNS

The professional lobbyists are, in effect, hired guns. "It matters little to these influence peddlars who wins elections," writes Al Hunt, of the *Wall Street Journal*. "Democratic lobbyists now brag about their Republican partners, and Republican lobbyists now brag about their Democratic partners."[3]

Many professionals don't care which side of an issue they're working for either: business or labor, environmentalists or polluters, Americans or foreigners. They'll work for anyone willing to pay their fee.

Why are the special interests willing to shell out large sums of money—often hundreds of thousands of dollars—for professional lobbyists' help? After all, anyone can demonstrate in favor of a cause he or she believes in. Anyone can call a congressperson's office or write a letter to a senator. With persistence, many constituents can find a way to talk to their representatives. Why should special interests hire professional lobbyists to do what their members can do themselves? The answer is that the professionals have certain advantages that ordinary citizens don't have.

By far the biggest of these advantages is clout—that

is, the ability to reach the people who count, the people who make the decisions that determine what the government does or doesn't do.

Many professional lobbyists are former government officials who once served in the House or Senate or in important positions in the White House. They know the people who occupy those positions now. What's more, they know how the government actually works. They know how to get things done, whom to talk to, who can get a particular bill moved through an important committee or get a particular government regulation reconsidered. They know what kind of argument, or what level of political pressure, will make that key person respond. This is knowledge that ordinary citizens—the grass roots lobbyists—don't have. And even if they did, they wouldn't have the clout to get through to the key person to make that vital argument or to apply that necessary pressure.

These advantages give professionals an enormously important place in the American political system. "Lobbying is as much a part of . . . democracy," says Jeff Birnbaum of the *Wall Street Journal,* "as any other branch of government."[4] Lobbyists, of course, are not actually a branch of government. But they are so powerful that Birnbaum's slip of the tongue—if that is what it was—is understandable.

It seems obvious to critics, from Ralph Nader to Jerry Brown, that professional lobbyists are far *too* important in the American political system, that they are a corrupting influence. Some cynics even believe that some of the high-priced Washington lobbyists peddle more than influence, that they actually buy and sell votes. They *must* be able to deliver votes for a price, these cynics charge. Otherwise why would their clients pay such huge sums to hire them?

The lobbyists insist that they don't sell votes, or even

influence. Instead, they claim to sell only what they call "access"—that is, what others call clout. In many cases, this may be true. There is little evidence of out-and-out bribery by professional lobbyists. But even the ability to provide clout is enough to skew the political process away from true democracy, in which everyone has an equal voice, and toward those with enough money to hire the best lobbyists. And the best lobbyists don't come cheap.

IN DEFENSE OF THE SPECIAL INTERESTS

Defenders of the special interest groups argue that they actually promote democracy rather than undermine it. They point out that the U.S. political system is fundamentally adversarial. It assumes that groups of citizens will be in conflict and that they will elect a variety of officials to represent their different interests. It is the job of those representatives to debate, negotiate, compromise, and ultimately arrive at decisions that will be good for society as a whole. At every step in the process, citizens have the right to express their will and to petition their representatives for the causes they believe in. Special interest groups are an important way in which that vital communication is carried out.

Special interest groups, their defenders insist, give power to individuals who would otherwise be politically powerless: ordinary working people, defenseless children, elderly men and women, nature lovers. It is only through special interest groups, working on their behalf, that such people have the chance to exert real influence on the government—influence they could never wield on their own.

Ultimately, the defenders argue, everyone benefits from the activities of the special interests. We all buy things, so we're all represented by consumer groups who work to keep prices down. We are all getting older, and so benefit from the work of lobbyists for the elderly. We all live on the same planet, and so are represented by the environmental groups working to clean the air and preserve the world's wildlife and resources. Most of us have a job or depend on someone who does, so we are represented by groups that fight for the rights of workers. We all benefit from a healthy American economy, and so are represented by the special interests fighting to protect American industry. And so on.

Some groups—like Common Cause, Public Citizen, and the Moral Majority—actually claim to speak for the public interest itself. They argue that they represent the principles and values of the great majority of the American people.

THE TROUBLE WITH THE SPECIAL INTERESTS

Opponents of special interest groups argue that most of them do not really represent the needs of ordinary citizens at all. Instead, each one represents only the narrow needs and goals of a particular group of people. Even the so-called public interest groups are usually active only in a small range of issues, and each tends to have a particular political point of view. Common Cause and Public Citizen, for example, generally support liberal causes. Conservatives are offended when these groups claim to represent them. On the other hand, liberals are equally offended by conservative groups like the Moral Majority and the Eagle Forum, which claim to represent the moral values of ordinary Americans.

The problem with the special interests, the critics complain, is that a democratic government is supposed to act on behalf of all the people. It is not supposed to favor one group, or even several groups, over the general interest. And yet, that is what special interest groups press the government to do. They want their own needs met, whatever effect that might have on society as a whole.

Some critics believe that the most powerful special interests—groups like the National Association of Manufacturers and the NRA—are so good at promoting their goals that they are a danger to the democratic process itself. Among these critics is Bill Clinton, who as a presidential candidate in 1992 named "the influence of organized interest groups" as the greatest single problem facing American democracy.[5]

Clinton is not the first president to warn against the special interests. More than two hundred years ago, James Madison spoke against groups "united and actuated by some common impulse of passion, or of interest, adverse to the rights of other citizens, or to the permanent and aggregate interests of the community."[6]

Special interest groups don't see themselves this way, of course. They deny that they seek advantages at the expense of the rest of society. Instead, each sees itself as a vital, functioning element of that society. What's good for them, they feel, is good for everyone else in the long run. They see the national interest and their interest as the same. "What is good for the country is good for General Motors," the president of General Motors, Charles Erwin Wilson, once told the Senate Armed Forces Committee. "And what's good for General Motors is good for the country."

In most cases, however, what's good for one interest group is bad for some other group, and often for society as a whole. Consider the question of taxes. Virtually every special interest group wants to see its own taxes reduced or eliminated. Business wants lower corporate taxes, consumers want lower sales taxes, homeowners want lower property taxes, and so on.

Now, no one likes to pay taxes, but we all know that

the expenses of government must be paid and that the money to pay them must come from taxes. We differ about how much money the government should spend, but we know that it has to spend something and that the money has to come from somewhere. The less *we* pay in taxes, the more *someone else* has to pay. When special interest groups are successful at getting their own taxes lowered, everyone else has to pay a greater share.

At least to some extent, then, special interest groups can be seen as working against the interests of society in general, because they seek advantages for themselves regardless of the effect on society as a whole, and because some of them do it so effectively.

Some special interest groups are far more powerful than others. Groups like the American Medical Association, the National Rifle Association, and the big unions exert much more influence than environmental groups and the organizations seeking aid for the homeless. This means that the interests of some Americans are much more effectively represented than are the interests of others. And the interest group that's most poorly represented is the public as a whole.

It takes a lot of money to play the lobbying game well; and the special interest groups that have a lot of money to spend are the ones that represent the wealthy and powerful, not the ones that work on behalf of the general public. According to political writer William Greider, public interest groups are often "outnumbered ten-to-one by industry interests" when government committees meet to decide on regulations for industry. "On some important matters, industry would invest fifty to one hundred times more resources than the public-interest advocates could muster."[7]

When there is a powerful special interest group working on one side of an issue and *only* the public interest on the other side, the special interest will probably triumph. That is because none of the thousands of special interest groups effectively represent the general interest in the same determined way.

"You know how [the U.S. political system] really works?" asks the conservative columnist Mona Charen. "It works for the benefit of the powerful and the wealthy."[8] They are the ones who can afford to hire the most influential lobbyists, and exert the most pressure on nervous politicians.

"THE MOTHER'S MILK OF POLITICS"

At one time, out-and-out bribery was a widespread problem in American politics. Large sums of money went from the hands of people seeking government favors into the pockets of politicians. The politicians did the favor and used the money to buy new cars or put their kids through college. This kind of corruption is probably not nearly as common as it used to be. But, according to many political observers, it has been replaced by another kind of financial corruption on a much bigger scale.

The power of the special interests rests on the power of money. When Jerry Brown charged that the American democratic system had been taken over, he explained that money was the "lubricant greasing the deal. Incredible sums—literally hundreds of millions of dollars—from political action committees (PACs), lobbyists and wealthy patrons have flooded into the campaign war chests of Washington's entrenched political elite—Democrats and Republicans alike."[1]

"Money," goes an old saying, "is the mother's milk of politics." Many critics think of it as a less than nourishing drink, a poison coursing through the political system, which may eventually destroy it altogether.

Why is money so important to U.S. politics? The over-
whelming reason is the incredible cost of election campaigns. Running for national office requires enormous
amounts of money. House races often cost many hundreds
of thousands of dollars. In 1992, some $678 million was
spent by House and Senate candidates, up roughly 50
percent from what was spent in 1990.[2]

The average Senate race costs $3 million, while a
race in a big state like California may run as high as $20
million. The *Washington Post* estimates that a typical
Senator needs to raise $12,000 a week, every week of his
or her Senate term, just in order to finance a reelection
campaign.[3] This puts tremendous economic pressure on
the politicians.

The great cost of campaigns gives wealthy candidates a tremendous advantage. Candidates can spend as
much of their own money as they choose, whereas candidates without enormous personal wealth have to raise
enormous amounts of money.

This difference is particularly important for first-
time candidates and challengers attempting to unseat incumbents. Incumbents have certain advantages when it
comes to raising money. They find it easier to attract
money from special-interest groups and others who hope
they will support the causes dear to their hearts. Such
groups are more inclined to contribute to incumbents than
to challengers because they consider the incumbents better bets. Historically, most incumbents are reelected.

One result of the enormous cost of senatorial campaigns is that the Senate is made up largely of people with
great personal wealth. It has sometimes been called a
millionaires' club, and with good reason. Several of the
current senators got to Washington by spending millions
of their own dollars on their first campaign. This is less

true of the House, but even there, many of the representatives had to spend a great deal of their own money on their first campaign. Citizens who don't have that kind of money to spend have a much slimmer chance of successfully running for office.

Once elected, even the wealthiest members of Congress need to find other sources of money to finance their campaigns for reelection. Even a great personal fortune could not support the repeated campaigns needed for a long career in Congress.

FUND-RAISING

Candidates raise money in a variety of ways. The most common is soliciting contributions from individuals and organizations. In the past, such large contributions were recognized as a major source of corruption. After all, it was sometimes hard to tell the difference between a large campaign contribution and a bribe. Because of this concern, laws were passed to regulate campaign contributions.

Individuals are now forbidden to give more than $1,000 to any one candidate in an election, no more than $20,000 to a political party campaign committee, and no more than $5,000 to a PAC. But politicians find many ways to disguise campaign contributions or to call them by other names.

Among other things, they stage events that supporters pay high prices to attend, with the money going to the candidate's campaign. Typical fund-raising events include dinners at which the candidate or some major political figure speaks, and special performances by entertainers who support the candidate.

A fund-raiser for an unknown congressional candidate might be held in a party room at a local hotel, with supporters paying five or ten dollars apiece to attend. Drinks and hors d'oeuvres are available, while the candidate mingles with the crowd, shaking hands and exchanging a few words with everyone. Such an affair might raise less than a thousand dollars altogether. On the other end of the political scale, a wealthy individual will pay many times that total just to eat a meal and sit near a powerful public official. This kind of fund-raising dinner might raise millions of dollars in a single night.

Among the biggest fund-raisers are those that feature a sitting president. People like to be in the same room with the president. In one month, April 1992, the Republican Campaign Committee raised $9 million from events providing this kind of access to President Bush.[4] Over four thousand people paid $1,500 each to attend a single dinner with the president. The dinner was held by a Republican Party committee rather than by the Bush campaign itself. Contributors who bought ten tickets (worth $15,000) got to sit at a table with a Republican representative. Those who bought twenty got a senator. Those who bought sixty tickets (worth about $90,000) had their picture taken with the president.[5] A similar event run by the Democrats—who didn't have a president as a drawing card—raised about one-third as much.

Donations like these, made to a political party or other political organization instead of directly to the candidate's campaign, are not limited by the legal restrictions on individual donations. "Despite . . . campaign-reform attempts," says *U.S. News & World Report,* "big contributors remain a driving force in politics."[6]

——— POLITICAL ACTION COMMITTEES ———

Political action committees, or PACs, were designed as a way for special interests to funnel contributions into election campaigns. In essence, they allow people or groups with common interests to pool their resources to support candidates. One advantage to PACs is that they allow individuals to make more politically meaningful contributions. Individual workers, for example, might be able to contribute only a small amount to candidates who support the cause of organized labor. But by forming a PAC unions can contribute a much larger and more significant amount. So can business organizations, minorities, environmentalists, doctors, and other special interest groups.

Under a 1974 federal law, each PAC must contribute to at least five candidates in federal elections, and must contribute no more than $5,000 to any candidate. Candidates can, however, receive as much as $5,000 each from an unlimited number of PACs.

Over half of all House members raise more than half of their campaign money from PACs.[7] This clearly makes PACs extremely important to them. It is not cynical to suspect that the politicians are grateful for this money and aware of where it comes from and of the interests those PACs represent. This gives those interests clout with the politicians and more influence than any of the individuals would have donating on their own.

Say four hundred people who favor gun control contribute ten dollars each to a House member's reelection campaign. Four thousand dollars is a significant amount of money and will no doubt be very useful to the campaign. The individual donations are so small that they—and the cause the donors believe in—would probably not even be noticed by the candidate. But if those donations are pooled and the $4,000 is given in one lump sum by a single person on behalf of a PAC, chances are that the donor will have a chance to talk to the representative and at least make the case for gun control.

Not everyone who contributes to a PAC or other fund-raising organization does so willingly. Union members have sometimes complained that their union fees are used for PACs that contribute money to candidates they oppose. In 1992, a Wisconsin man named William Neiss charged in court that his employer had pressured him to pay $1,500 for tickets to a fund-raising dinner for the Bush campaign. Neiss claimed that he was fired when he refused to contribute.[8] The company denied it, but Neiss's claim echoed the charges of many other workers and executives who feel forced to contribute to political causes supported by their employers or by their unions.

As this book is being written, a law is being considered in Congress that would try to reduce the influence of the special interests by eliminating PACs altogether. Most observers doubt that the law will pass, and even if it does, they doubt that its passage will make much difference.

Doing away with PACs won't solve the problem, says Candice Nelson, author of *The Money Chase*, a book about the effect of money on the political system. If the bill does pass, Nelson says, "It may actually lead to a less desirable system than we have now."[9]

PACs are only one of the devices used by special interests to channel their money into political campaigns. If they are eliminated, new devices will be found. At best, says Peggy Connolly, who served as press director for presidential candidate Paul Tsongas in 1992, fund-raising reforms mean "a delay in the time it takes people to figure out loopholes in the system."[10]

The reality is that the money is needed. It has to come from somewhere, and it is the wealthy contributors and the special interests who have it to give. Politicians will always find some way to get it, not because they want to, but because they have to.

The alternatives to PACs may well be worse. "The only [other] way a candidate can raise big money now is to run around the country temporarily convincing everyone you speak with that you're on their side," says Connolly. "Then you disappoint many of them after the election."[11]

The less that wealthy individuals and PACs contribute, the more citizens will have to be "temporarily convinced" of untruths, and the more temptation there will be for candidates to lie.

THE CORRUPTING EFFECTS OF MONEY

Mark Twain once described the U.S. Congress as the best legislature that money can buy. Along with many other critics since, Twain recognized that money has a corrupting influence on the entire political process.

It is probably rare today for people to tell congresspersons or senators that they will give them so much money in return for a particular vote. That is not the way it works. But politicians are constantly aware of which votes—and which positions on which issues—will win them the support of major contributors, and which will not. However much they deny it, this is bound to affect their behavior in office.

Most politicians probably want to be honest, and most try very hard to behave honorably. It may be that most congresspersons would refuse to do anything they considered illegal, or clearly improper. It may even be that most would never cast a vote they were convinced was bad for the country. It is in the borderline cases— the gray areas where politicians can convince themselves that it doesn't matter very much what they do—that the corrupting power of money most often works its harm.

It's not just the actual need for money that causes the problem. Getting a contribution from a PAC or from a wealthy contributor can be useful for a successful politician, but not getting it is rarely a disaster. After all, there are thousands of PACs and many more thousands of potential contributors. If one doesn't contribute to your campaign, another might. The real fear is that the PAC, and the special interest it represents, will support your opponent. Often, then, the politicians don't try so much to please the special interests as they try not to anger them. Either way, the constant worry about money distracts politicians from what should be their major concern: the welfare and security of the nation as a whole.

No matter how honest individual politicians may be, they cannot afford to ignore the power of money over their political future. Their need for money is continuous, and they are bound to be grateful to whoever supplies it. How can a senator who needs $500,000 for television ads by next month fail to be friendly when a potential contributor drops by to discuss a bill before her committee? How can a congressman facing a tough fight for reelection ignore a wealthy business owner who wants him to talk to a regulatory agency on behalf of her regulated business?

Some politicians argue that there is nothing essentially corrupting about large gifts of campaign money. "Generally," says Republican senator Orrin Hatch, of Utah, the donations come from "people who agree with you. Generally, you agree with them. So it isn't a matter of being corrupted by having them help you."[12]

But critics like maverick presidential candidate Ross Perot disagree. Politicians may not want to be corrupted—they may not even think that they are being corrupted—but they can't help it. "They are all nice people," Perot acknowledges. "I don't think there are any villains. But, boy, is the system rotten."[13]

SIX

GOVERNMENT BY OBSTRUCTION

The U.S. government was founded by people who distrusted the power of government. This distrust led them to design a political system based on obstruction, a system in which it is easier to stop something from being done than to do it.

Cooperation and compromise are needed to get much done much under this system, but they are becoming hard to find.

RIVALRIES

As we have seen, the two parties sometimes obstruct each other for political advantage. But partisanship is not the only obstacle to governmental cooperation. There is also a growing tension between the branches of government and even between agencies of the same branch.

The FBI, the Federal Bureau of Alcohol, Tobacco and Firearms, and the U.S. Customs Bureau, for example, often battle over turf and credit for victories in the struggle against smugglers. Congressional committees are often at odds over which should have jurisdiction over important bills. Even within the judicial branch, courts often quarrel with each other. Recently the U.S. Supreme Court itself got so angry with the federal courts in California that it ordered them to stop granting so many stays of execution to condemned criminals.

But the rivalry may be most intense of all between the two branches of Congress, and between Congress and the president. This rivalry has always been there, explains the conservative columnist George Will. The founders designed the branches that way. But, he adds, "I believe the rivalry is exceptionally bitter these days."[1] These branches of government, and the people who run them, seem to have less and less tolerance and respect for each other.

Partly this has to do with politics. All presidents since Jimmy Carter have been elected after campaigning against "Washington"—that is, against Congress. This has led many representatives and senators to welcome them to Washington with suspicion and dislike.

Many Democratic congresspeople had an actual contempt for President Ronald Reagan. Although they respected and feared his political power and popularity, they privately suggested that he was neither as intelligent nor as sophisticated as a president should be. In private, they told of his reading from note cards in conversations with them and of his nodding off to sleep in important conferences.

President George Bush spent much of his presidency blaming what he called the "Democrat Congress" for the country's troubles, and he used the presidential veto to block more bills than any other president in history. And even Bill Clinton—the first president in twelve years to have both houses of Congress controlled by his own party—has not been able to count on the support of Congress for his proposals.

A certain amount of tension is bound to exist between the legislative and executive branches. But like George Will, Howard Baker, the one-time Republican majority leader of the U.S. Senate, believes that the present hostility goes beyond traditional politics. It has become a real personal "antipathy," says Baker, an enmity that Baker believes has become dangerously "corrosive" to the system itself.[2]

THE DIFFICULTY OF GETTING A BILL THROUGH CONGRESS

Congress is the machine that transforms the people's will into the laws that govern the country. And nowhere in the government is obstruction easier than in the Congress.

Passing a major bill through Congress is a complicated and difficult process. A bill can be proposed in either house of Congress or in both houses at once. It is then referred to at least one committee in each house. Either the whole committee or a smaller part of it, known as a subcommittee, then marks up the bill, determining the form in which it will be presented to the full house. All together there are about 278 committees and subcommittees in Congress, one or more of which will have responsibility for every major bill. Many bills are killed in committee and never reach the floor at all. Others come out of committee drastically different from the original proposal.

In the House of Representatives, every bill then must go through the Rules Committee, which decides, among other things, how much time will be given to the bill on the House floor and whether it will be open to amendments.

Only after all this is the bill debated and voted on by the whole house in which it was proposed. Once it has passed one house of Congress, it must be passed by the other. Even then the bill is not ready to become law. Amendments have usually been added by each house, either in committee or on the floor. Some of these amendments change the nature of the bill. Others have nothing to do with the subject matter of the original bill at all. Because the House and the Senate have passed different versions of the bill, it then has to be referred to a conference committee made up of members of both houses.

This committee has the job of reconciling the two versions of the bill and coming up with a final bill acceptable to both houses. Depending on the nature of the bill, this committee may be either small or large. The committee assigned to reconcile the the 1993 budget bill had 228 members—more than twice as many legislators as there are in the entire Senate!

The version of the bill arrived at by the reconciliation committee is then returned to each house for a final vote. Even after surviving all this, the bill still has to go to the president for approval. If the president vetoes the bill instead, it will take the vote of two-thirds of both houses of Congress to pass it into law.

———— THE POWER OF A TANTRUM ————

In one respect, nothing could be more democratic than this torturous process. It is a basic ideal of democratic government that the rights of the minority must be protected. Checks and balances that make it relatively easy to block rash or unjust actions of the government help minorities to protect themselves.

But in another respect, the ease with which government action can be aborted is profoundly undemocratic in that it allows for a minority in certain instances to thwart the will of the majority. Sometimes it is even possible for a single stubborn member of the majority party to do so.

As we have seen, the Republicans in Congress were solidly united against President Clinton's 1993 budget plan. They could not, however, defeat it on their own, since the Democrats had a majority in both houses of Congress. That meant that every Democratic vote became tremendously important, and every Democratic senator held a kind of veto power over the bill. "All a Democratic senator has to do," explained journalist Eleanor Clift, "is throw a tantrum and he'll get what he wants" out of the budget bill.[3] "Any one Democratic senator has the power to veto the president's whole economic package," agreed another veteran Washington journalist, Cokie Roberts.[4]

The one who used that power most effectively was Herbert Kohl of Wisconsin. Senator Kohl didn't like the size of a tax on gasoline that the administration had proposed to lower the federal deficit. In the House-Senate conference on the budget, Kohl insisted that he wouldn't vote for the bill if the gas tax wasn't cut to 4.3 cents a gallon. Other Democrat senators insisted that that was too little to make a real difference to the deficit. Nonetheless, the bill came out of the conference with a mere 4.3 cents a gallon tax on gasoline. "The Senate must bow to Herbert Kohl's wishes," explained Roberts, "because the president needs Herbert Kohl's vote."[5]

The Democrats, of course, blamed the Republicans for the situation. They accused them of stubbornly refusing to cooperate in the budget process. The Republicans, on the other hand, blamed the Democrats for being so weak and disorganized that they allowed a relatively obscure senator like Kohl to dictate Senate policy. The Democrats seemed determined to prove the truth of humorist Will Rogers's old line: "I don't belong to any organized political party. I'm a Democrat."

Whoever was to blame, few people of either party argued that this was the way the system should work. A single first-term senator should not have the power to determine the fate of an important element of the national budget by "throwing a tantrum."

A RECIPE FOR PORK

The budget debate of 1993 was an unusual situation. It is rare for either party, Republican or Democrat, to be as united as the Republicans were then. And it is equally rare for either party to totally withdraw from the process of negotiating such an important measure as the budget. But it is far from rare for a single senator or representative to control the fate of an important measure.

Among other things, the legislative process is a recipe for pork. That is because it is relatively easy for a handful of legislators, or even a single key legislator, to alter or block passage of an entire bill. The chairman of the markup committee, for example, often has the power to determine whether a bill will reach the floor. Even if it does reach the floor, passage may depend on a few legislators who could vote either way. These swing voters often have no real interest in this bill itself. But they *are* interested in other matters. In order to win their votes, irrelevant provisions are added to many bills.

These so-called pork barrel measures are the products of a kind of negotiation and compromise that amounts to legislative blackmail. "If you want my support for your bill," the swing legislator implies, "you must give me something in return." Typically what is given is a provision that uses taxpayers' money to benefit constituents in the legislator's state or district—a highway-building project that will provide jobs in a congressperson's district, or a space research contract for a major university in a senator's home state. Pork adds to the cost of many bills—and to the federal debt. It also adds to the anger and frustration many citizens feel about their government.

A DESIGN FOR GRIDLOCK

All this amounts to a design for governmental paralysis. "We have a system here which perpetuates gridlock," complains Representative Vic Fazio, a Democrat from California. It "allows each party to have its moment but never to accomplish its purpose."[6]

Others, like former vice president Dan Quayle, enjoy the fact that it is difficult to get things done. "From my conservative viewpoint and my conservative ideology, the more Congress is messed up, the better off the country is," says Quayle.[7] Quayle and other conservatives believe, with Thomas Jefferson, that the government should do as little as possible.

At least part of the fault for gridlock—if it is a fault—lies in the structure of the government. The checks and balances built into the system may help keep the government from acting rashly or dictatorially, but they can keep it from acting sensibly as well.

At best, controversial measures are endlessly compromised before they are even voted on in Congress. At worst, they are dropped altogether. Some that do pass are undercut by countermeasures that weaken or offset them. Any measure proposed by the president is likely to be chipped and chopped away at, first by one house, then by the other, and finally by a conference committee made up of members from both houses.

What's more, the fact that no one—and no branch of government—has the power to act alone means that no one is clearly accountable for what is done, or for what is left undone. And no one is fully responsible when things go wrong. The Democrats blame the Republicans. The Republicans blame the Democrats. The House blames the Senate. The Senate blames the House. Both blame the president. The president blames them. And so on, around and around.

"[The people] long for a clear authority," says Jim Squires, a widely respected political consultant who worked for Ross Perot in his 1992 campaign.[8] They want some person or party who can take charge, who can get things done. As it is, no one seems to have that kind of authority. Worse, no one seems to want it.

TO LEAD OR
TO FOLLOW?

We speak of our elected officials as "leaders." We look to them, and particularly to the president, to point the direction for the country to go, and to guide us along the way. But it often seems that leading is the last thing most politicians want to do. They are far more comfortable following public opinion than leading it.

It can be argued that this is exactly the way things should be. Ours is a representative form of government. Senators and congresspeople speak—and vote—for their constituents as well as for themselves. Perhaps their sole function should be to determine what their constituents want, and to vote accordingly.

Do our politicians need to be leaders at all?

—————— WHO DO REPRESENTATIVES —————— REPRESENT?

What are the duties of the representatives? Whom do they represent? Elected representatives are constantly faced with this question. It has no easy answer.

Take an imaginary U.S. congresswoman named Jane Smith.

Officially, she is the representative from the Seventh

District of the state of New Heartland. This implies that she represents the entire district and everyone in it. But some of the voters of the district voted for her, some voted against her, and some didn't vote at all. Does she have some special duty to the voters who supported her? Or does she represent everyone in the district equally?

What about the people of the rest of the state? And the rest of the country? She serves, after all, in the Congress of the United States, not the Congress of New Heartland. Her actions affect everyone in the entire country, not just the people of her home district. What duty does she owe to the people of New York, of Oregon, of Mississippi, of Iowa?

She has no problem when the interests of the people of her district and the interests of the country are the same. The trouble comes when interests conflict. And in a democracy interests always conflict.

Say that a large government research project is based in the Seventh District of New Heartland. The project employs two thousand people and brings more than $2 billion dollars to the state each year. New Heartland is a small, poor state. The money the project brings in is vital to the state's economy.

But the project carries out large-scale experiments that injure the local environment and destroy thousands of acres of forest and farmland. What's more, it has become increasingly obvious that the research project is a failure. In the opinion of independent experts, it is scientifically useless. Critics insist that the whole thing is a waste of money and should be shut down.

A bill to end the project is introduced in the Congress. What should Congresswoman Smith and her fellow representatives from New Heartland do? Should they fight to keep the project alive, or should they vote to kill it?

In the last election, the most active interest groups in New Heartland were the environmentalists. They supported all three of the winning representatives, considering them better on environmental issues than their opponents. The environmentalists not only contributed large amounts of money to all three campaigns, they went from door to door on the candidates' behalf, making a big difference in getting them elected. The environmentalists favor closing down the project. What's more, it's clear that doing away with the project would be in the best interest of the taxpayers of the entire country, saving them billions of dollars in tax money.

On the other hand, shutting down the project would immediately throw two thousand New Heartland residents out of work. Even worse, it would devastate the economy of a large part of the state, an area that includes parts of all three districts, and which depends heavily on the income earned by the people working on the project. Hundreds of businesses would have to close, and many thousands more people would eventually lose their jobs.

Federal officials face this kind of conflict between local and national interests all the time, and they resolve it in different ways. Let's see how the three representatives from New Heartland will respond.

Representative Smith always tries to follow the will of the majority of the people of her district, regardless of who supported her and who did not. Because the project is in the Seventh District, she will put the interests of the people of her district ahead of the interests of her environmentalist supporters and of the nation as a whole. She will fight to keep the project going.

Representative Bill Brown has a different view of his responsibility. He believes that he owes his main allegiance to the people who supported and voted for him. Because the environmentalists gave him the strongest support in the election, he will support them now. Although many people in his district may be economically harmed by his decision and may vote against him in the next election because of it, Congressman Brown will vote against the project.

Representative Sam Jones sees himself not as representing a particular group or region but as representing the country as a whole. Because it is in the financial interest of the vast majority of American taxpayers, he will vote to kill the project.

Which of the three representatives is right? Which has the best vision of democracy? That is up to each representative, and each voter, to decide.

INDEPENDENT JUDGMENT

Some citizens assume that the job of a representative is to act as a proxy for the people back home—that is, to do what the constituents would do if they were in Washington themselves. These people get very upset when their representative or senator votes differently than they would have voted if they'd had the chance. They feel betrayed.

But, as we have seen, many representatives see their responsibilities differently. They argue that they can't possibly vote the way every one of their constituents wants them to vote, since their constituents disagree with one another.

They can, however, vote the way the *majority* of their constituents want them to vote, which would seem to follow the democratic ideal of majority rule. But to do so, some argue, would make them nothing more than pollsters. Why have a Congress at all if the members simply read the latest polls and vote accordingly? They believe that representatives are elected to do much more than that. They believe that their duty is to represent, not the people's *wishes,* but the people's *best interest.* And to do that, they must use their own judgment, knowledge, and experience to decide what that best interest really is and how to achieve it.

The great eighteenth-century British politician Edmund Burke expressed this idea of the representative more than two centuries ago. "It is [the representative's] duty to sacrifice his repose, his pleasure, his satisfactions, to [his constituents]—and above all, ever, and in all cases, to prefer their interests to his own," declared Burke. "But his unbiased opinion, his mature judgment, his enlightened conscience, he ought not to sacrifice to [them], to any man, or to any set of men living. . . . Your representative owes you, not his industry only, but his judgment; and he betrays, instead of serving you, if he sacrifices it to your opinion."[1]

Politicians who follow Burke's advice will sometimes support measures the public at large does not approve. In that case, they insist, it is the representatives' duty to lead: to act decisively to do what they are convinced is best for the country and, ultimately, to take the consequences of that action. If the public remains unconvinced, or if the controversial measures fail, then the representative can expect to be thrown out of office at the next election. That, Burke would argue, is the price that must be paid for leadership in a democracy.

In the United States today, however, few politicians are willing to pay that price. Or even to risk having to pay it.

_____ GOVERNMENT BY HORSE RACE _____

"Winning isn't everything," coach Vince Lombardi is alleged to have said. "It's the only thing." Lombardi was talking about professional football, but many politicians feel the same way about politics. For them, winning elections is the only thing. Running the country may be more important than running down the field with a football, but the object is still to win.

From the moment many victorious candidates take

office for the first time, they are planning the next election. Every step they take in government is determined by its potential effect on the next election. If I do this, will the voters approve? Will it please my financial supporters? If I do that, will it anger an important special interest? Will it hurt fund-raising for my next campaign?

Nothing else seems to matter quite so much. Political beliefs, moral ideals, even personal relationships—all are sacrificed to the goal of winning. "If you want a friend in Washington," said President Harry Truman, "get a dog." It had better be a small dog, adds the *Washington Times* editor, Wes Pruden. "Even he might turn on you."[2]

Among the many things that run second to the needs of their political careers are the needs of the country. Virtually every political issue is considered less on its merits than on its effect on the next election. What's the most popular position to take? Which position will help me with the most voters, or hurt me with the fewest? What's best for the country often seems of much less interest than the what's most politically advantageous. A sign hanging on the wall of the headquarters of the Republican National Convention said it all. "Great idea," proclaimed the sign, but "does it get us any votes?"

And it's not only the politicians who become obsessed with winning. In the media, political campaigns are covered almost like extended athletic events. The "story," in journalistic terms, is the horse race. Who's ahead? Is the leader gaining or slipping in the polls? What the election of Candidate X or Candidate Y would mean for the country hardly seems to matter. All that counts is which one is going to win.

————————— NO NEED TO LEAD —————————

Many Washington observers were surprised when Senator John Sherman Cooper voted for the Civil Rights Bill in

1964. Cooper was a Republican from Kentucky, and the bill, which granted a variety of civil rights to African Americans, was extremely unpopular with Kentucky voters. But despite the political price he seemed certain to pay, Cooper did what he—not his voters—thought was right. "You don't just wet your finger and see which way the wind blows," Cooper explained. "They send you here to lead."[3]

Cooper's political courage was impressive. But what was even more notable was the surprise with which it was met by veteran political observers. Such independence and courage were rare in 1964, and they have been getting even rarer in recent years.

Leadership often requires proposing new and sometimes daring solutions to difficult problems. And yet—no matter how serious the problem, and no matter how often the usual ways of dealing with the problem have failed—most politicians are reluctant to propose new and potentially unpopular solutions. They're even reluctant to vote for them.

It is hard for many officeholders to vote for controversial bills—bills that would cut popular programs, for example, or raise taxes—even when they're convinced that those measures would be good for the country. When it comes to a tough bill, says Lloyd Bentsen the secretary of the Treasury, "The easiest thing to do is to vote no and then hope that it passes" without you.[4] If enough timid politicians do this, of course, the bill will fail.

The safest thing for a politician to do is to find out what the people think and go along with it. And thanks to the effectiveness of modern polling techniques, this is a relatively easy thing to do. "No political leader needs to guess at what the people think about any issue," explains Republican political consultant Doug Bailey. "[T]herefore there is no need ever to go out and lead."[5]

One thing the politicians learn from the polls is that

they're not likely to get reelected by backing controversial measures. Some voters, attracted by the proposals, may take a chance and vote for you. But their support is likely to be tentative and halfhearted. After all, no one can be sure that an untried proposal will work. Meanwhile, other voters will be truly alarmed. They are the people who like things the way they are: the ones who profit from the status quo, along with the ones who are simply terrified of change. And fear will make them active. They won't just vote against you, they'll *work* against you. They'll organize support for your opponent and do everything they can to keep you from changing things.

Knowing this, a politician becomes afraid. He or she begins to rationalize. It would be nice to take a stand here, he thinks, to raise the tough issues and really try to accomplish something. But if I do, I might not be reelected. And if I'm not, I won't be able to accomplish anything in the future. Maybe it's better not to rock the boat.

THE COUNTRY'S NEED FOR LEADERSHIP

Politicians may have no need to lead, but the nation has a desperate need for leadership. Most ordinary citizens have little time or desire to study the nation's problems. They are not experts in economics or history or politics, and they have little understanding of the way the government actually works. That is why they need representatives to deal with those problems for them. It is up to these representatives to study the issues, to debate them, and finally to decide how to deal with them. It is their job to point out the direction in which the country should move, and to lead the people along that path. If the politicians refuse to take the lead, who will?

What can be done to make elected officials face up to

the nation's problems? "Somebody's got to break that chain," says Democratic senator Sam Nunn of Georgia. "Some people are just going to have to be willing to be beaten."[6] Nunn, it should be mentioned, has been in the Senate since 1972 and has shown little willingness to risk being beaten himself.

MISREPRESENTATION

The same fear that makes politicians timid and reluctant to lead often makes them lie. The fact that politicians lie is a serious problem in a democracy—and not just because people don't like being lied to.

Another word for a lie is "misrepresentation." And in fact, lying by politicians undermines the essential principle of representative government. If voters don't know the truth about what a politician is doing, or even what the politician believes in, how can they decide whether they want him or her to represent them?

———————— WHY POLITICIANS LIE ————————

There's no mystery about why politicians lie to voters. Sometimes they do it to cover up illegal or immoral behavior. But most of the time they lie to get—or not to lose—votes.

The fact that politicians lie to voters is not entirely the politicians' fault. It's the voters' fault as well. Fear of losing office is really fear of the voter. And the politicians have good reason to be afraid. "An honest politician may—by accident—get elected," says Sam Fullwood III, a political reporter for the *Los Angeles Times*. "But they'll never get reelected."[1]

Veteran political observers like Fullwood believe that voters put unrealistic demands on their representatives. The same voters who complain that their politicians lie to them insist that the politicians do so as the price for receiving their votes.

Politicians are human beings, with all the faults and weaknesses that every human being has. Deep down, most voters probably know this. And yet many voters demand that their representatives present themselves as morally upright and unfailingly idealistic.

Getting elected takes enormous amounts of money, and yet many voters expect their representatives to pretend not to care about money.

Running a government requires politicians to make many deals and compromises, and yet many voters expect their representatives to be unyielding.

Voters tend to be intolerant of politicians who tell the truth about what they are doing behind the closed doors of government—or even about what they believe needs to be done. As we have seen, completely honest political leadership would often require politicians to support unpopular measures, and yet voters tend to reject any politician who does that. This is why politicians find it easier, and safer, to lie.

—————— BROKEN PROMISES ——————

Political candidates routinely mislead voters about what they will do when they get into office. They promise the voters things they either cannot deliver or have no intention of delivering.

In 1992, presidential candidate Bill Clinton took several strong stands on issues and made several specific promises about what he would do if he was elected president.

For instance, he attacked President Bush's policy of

sending desperate escapees from the Caribbean island of Haiti, who claimed to be victims of political persecution, back to their country. Clinton promised that he would change that policy and review their cases on an individual basis. He also declared that he would use his presidential authority to lift the ban against homosexuals serving in the military. And he proposed a sweeping student-aid plan that would allow all qualified young people to attend the college of their choice in return for two years of public service.

And yet, once in office, Clinton continued President Bush's policy of returning Haitian refugees. Then, instead of immediately lifting the ban on homosexuals in the military, Clinton called for his secretary of defense and the Joint Chiefs of Staff to develop a new policy, which he eventually endorsed. The policy kept the ban in effect, although the military agreed to enforce it less aggressively than in the past. Instead of a sweeping new plan for financing college education, Clinton proposed a much less ambitious plan that offered only a small proportion of qualified students the opportunity to do public service in return for a small amount of student aid.

Bill Clinton is not the only modern president to disappoint his supporters by failing to fulfill his campaign promises. In 1968, Richard Nixon campaigned with a claim that he had a "secret plan" to end the unpopular War in Vietnam with honor and bring the American troops home. He was elected, but the war went on until 1973, and then ended under what many of Nixon's early supporters considered dishonorable terms.

Ronald Reagan promised to balance the federal budget in his first term by cutting taxes and government spending while at the same time greatly strenghtening the U.S. military. During his two terms in office, however, the national debt soared to historic heights.

George Bush promised that he would veto any

attempt to raise taxes. When skeptics suggested that he might have to go back on that promise once he was elected, Bush insisted that he would not do that under any circumstances. "Read my lips," he told a delighted crowd at the 1988 Republican Convention. "No new taxes." And yet, in 1990, Bush agreed to a plan that included the largest tax increase in history up to that time.

At least some of these presidents may not have intended to lie. They may have meant what they said when they said it. Nixon may have sincerely thought his Vietnam policy would succeed. Reagan may have actually believed that tax cuts for the wealthy and a new social welfare policy would wipe out the deficit. Clinton may have honestly changed his mind about what he should do with the Haitian refugees, and then Congress made it harder than he expected to launch a massive national service program and to transform the military's policy regarding homosexuals.

But, whether the lies were intentional or not, the result was the same. The people did not get what they voted for—and what they were deceived into expecting. That can be seen as a fundamental violation of democratic principles.

Politicians don't just lie about their activities and about what they do or plan to do. Many also lie about issues, telling the voters what they want to hear instead of what they need to know.

Former senator Paul Tsongas accuses both Republicans and Democrats of lying about what needs to be done to reduce the country's huge budget deficit.[2] The Republicans, says Tsongas, tell the voters that the deficit can be wiped out by cutting government spending and without raising taxes. The Democrats claim that it can be done by taxing only the wealthy. Both sides know better, says Tsongas. They, along with virtually all reputable economists, know that seriously reducing the deficit would take a combination of spending cuts and taxes on both the wealthy and the middle class. The lies—the misrepresentations—are deliberate.

Republicans lie because they can't get elected without the votes of large numbers of people who oppose any rise in taxes. Democrats lie because they can't be elected without appealing to voters who are hostile to the rich and who fear any rise in taxes on the middle class.

—————— TWISTING THE LANGUAGE ——————

Deception is built into the very language that politicians use to discuss important issues. Presidents don't send troops to war; they send them on "peace-keeping missions." Missiles don't mistakenly blow up hospitals and office buildings, killing innocent people; they inflict "collateral damage." Taxes are not raised; "revenues are enhanced."

Nowhere is politicians' language as willfully confusing as in discussing the politically sensitive issues of government spending and taxes. "Seasonally adjusted forecasts," "inflation-adjusted," "estimated shortfalls," "economic assumptions," "baselines"—terms like these are used by economists to explain economic reality to each other. They are used by politicians to hide economic reality from voters.

Perhaps the most glaring example of misleading political language is the way that politicians use the word "cut." To most people, a cut in spending means a reduction. But that is not what politicians mean by it. They repeatedly claim to be cutting spending on various programs, giving the impression that less money will be spent on them in the future. But all they are really talking about is increasing spending by less than they might have.

In order to understand this, let's say the government

spent $350 billion on national defense last year. A bill is proposed in Congress to spend $400 billion next year. An amendment is passed to spend $375 billion instead. In political language, that is referred to as a $25 billion spending *cut*. The politicians responsible will proudly claim that they have reduced defense spending by $25 billion. And yet, in reality, defense spending will be *increased* by $25 billion!

Some informed voters understand this, but many do not. They assume that the cuts politicians promise are actual *reductions* in spending, not just lowerings of predicted increases. These voters are inevitably angered and disillusioned when government spending continues to go up under both Republicans and Democrats, all of whom have continually promised to "cut" it.

Even those who understand this basic twisting of language are hopelessly confused by the jumble of numbers politicians toss around, all of which differ from each other and all of which are used in ways that are often deliberately meant to mislead the voters. Politicians can often use very different numbers without actually lying because the numbers are largely imaginary anyway. Most are estimates of what is likely to happen in the future, and politicians are free to be as optimistic or as gloomy in their predictions as they choose to be. Typically, those who are in power—whichever party they belong to—use one set of numbers to reassure the voters. Those on the outside use another set of numbers to alarm them.

SECRECY

Much of what the government does, it does in secret. This is particularly true when it comes to producing legislation. Although most of the proceedings of the House and Senate are public, and regular sessions are even shown live on television, much of the real work that goes into the writing of bills goes on in private. It is sometimes said that there are two things people should never watch being made: laws and sausages. The reason? Because if people saw what goes into either one they'd be so disgusted they'd never have anything to do with them again.

Legislators meet with one another in their offices, on golf courses, at health clubs, or over drinks or dinner. They talk about the issues involved in the bill, argue with each other, make deals and trade-offs. Lobbyists—who often know more about the issues than the legislators—meet with congresspeople and their staffs, pleading and cajoling and helping to shape the contents of bills. In some cases, lobbyists actually write parts of the bills, which sympathetic legislators then introduce under their own names.

Some critics argue that the secrecy in which bills are written is antidemocratic. The people need know what goes into the legislative sausage, say the critics, so that they can judge whether their representatives are really acting in their best interests. Secrecy only makes it easier for the special interests and their lobbyists to work their influence on lawmakers.

Defenders of the current system respond that a certain amount of secrecy is necessary for the legislative process to work. The nation's founders recognized this when they met in secret to write the Constitution, not even keeping detailed notes of their proceedings, much less releasing them to the public afterward.

The process of reaching agreement on a major bill usually involves a lot of deal-making and compromise, activities many voters disapprove of. Many citizens feel there is something wrong with representatives in effect trading their votes—agreeing to vote with a colleague on one bill, say, in return for the colleague's vote on another bill. Some disapprove of a representative voting in favor of any bill with which he or she does not totally agree.

And yet, if repesentatives refused to do these things, agreement could not be reached, laws could not be made, and the government could not function. It is probable that few representatives are ever happy with all the provisions of any bill. If each representative had to be personally satisfied with every aspect of a bill before voting for it, no bill would ever be passed.

A positive case for legislative secrecy was made by Democratic representative Anthony Beilenson of California before a hearing of the House Ways and Means Committee in 1992. He argued that there is already too much close scrutiny of politicians in the act of governing. They are already too afraid to do anything decisive because they know it is bound to anger some group or other. The more closely legislators are watched, the more their motives are publicly probed and picked over, the more frightened they will become, and the less they will accomplish.

"We're suffocating our form of government," warned Beilenson. "The only time the House Ways and Means Committee does anything good [for the country] is when they meet behind closed doors and then come out and lie about their votes."[3]

Besides, argue the defenders of the status quo. It's the results that matter. However secretly bills are written, they are eventually brought out into the open, examined in Congressional and Senate committee hearings that are usually open to the public, and debated publicly on the floors of both houses. The people can judge the legislators' work by the laws themselves. They don't need to know the details of the often messy, and sometimes gory, process that produced them.

OPENING UP
THE PROCESS

"Much of the strength and efficiency of any government
. . . depends on *opinion*," declared Benjamin Franklin.
"On the general opinion of the goodness of that government, as well as of the wisdom and integrity of its governors."[1]

By this key measure, the U.S. government is in
serious trouble. Public opinion is particularly important in
a democracy, where the people are supposed to rule. Yet,
the general opinion of the U.S. government and those who
run it is extremely low. According to a variety of recent
polls, neither the president nor the Congress nor the government as a whole commands the support of even half
the nation's citizens.

The greatest, most ambitious democratic experiment
in history has failed to keep the respect and trust of the
very people who are supposed to rule it. If it is to get them
back, the political system must be reformed to give those
people more actual control.

In the next two chapters, we will discuss some of the
reforms that are often suggested to open up the political
process and make it more democratic.

The first step reformers often suggest is not a reform of the political system at all. It is a reform of the way most of us use the system that already exists.

Many of the people who are most cynical about the political process don't even take part in it. They leave it to the politicians to operate the system as they see fit, then they complain about what the politicians do with it. No democracy can work if the people—who are at the heart of any democratic system—refuse to participate in it.

Political activists as varied as Ralph Nader, Ross Perot, and Jerry Brown encourage citizens to get more involved in the democratic process. You don't have to sit and complain from the sidelines, they tell citizens. You can take part in the system yourself. Write letters to the editors of your local newspapers. Write your representatives. Call them. Support candidates you agree with. Oppose candidates you dislike.

Nor should people be satisfied with acting as individuals. Those who worry that special-interest groups exert too much influence might consider the old axiom: If you can't lick 'em, join 'em. There are special-interest groups that support almost every cause imaginable: nuclear disarmament, lower taxes, prayer in the schools, an end to abortion, unrestricted abortion, gun control, abolition of the death penalty, greater use of the death penalty, absolute freedom of speech, censorship of pornography, and so on.

If your cause is *not* supported by any existing group, you can join with other people who agree with you to organize one. Joining or forming a special-interest group can help you exert as much influence as the current system allows.

ENCOURAGE THIRD (AND FOURTH ___ AND FIFTH) PARTIES

Nothing is more vital to a representative democracy than the election process. It is in elections that the people express their will and choose their leaders. The more open that process is, the more democratic the political system becomes.

As we have seen, the election process in the United States is dominated by the twin forces of the Republican and Democratic parties. What are people who fundamentally disagree with the Tweedledee and Tweedledum of the major political parties to do? Where can they go? What can be done about the stranglehold the two major parties have on American politics? What can be done to open up the process to new ideas, new politicians, and new arguments? One obvious answer to all these questions is to encourage the birth and development of new political parties.

Third parties have sometimes had invigorating effects on U.S. politics. Many of the most important sprang up in response to specific issues. The Free Soil Party, for example, was formed to oppose slavery, the Greenback Party to expand the supply of paper money. Policies that these and other third parties originally advanced have frequently been adopted by major parties and enacted into law. The Prohibition Party's temperance campaign led to the Eighteenth Amendment banning the sale of alcohol. Social Security was suggested by the Socialist Party long before it became a reality during the New Deal. And so on.

Despite their occasional influence, third parties have rarely had much success winning national office. The last one to become a major party was the Republican Party more than a century ago.

The last third-party presidential candidate to win

any electoral votes was George Wallace, who won 46 in 1968. Wallace, who appealed largely to die-hard southern segregationists and northerners angry about the civil rights movement and anti–Vietnam War protests, was an ex-Democrat who ran as the candidate of his own American Independent Party. By the next election, however, he had returned to the Democratic fold. John Anderson in 1980 and Ross Perot in 1992 each got millions of votes running as independents, but neither had a party behind him, and neither won any electoral votes.

There are plenty of third, or minor, parties around today, on both the political Right and Left. Most are too extreme to win widespread support any time soon. In the wake of the 1992 elections, however, there has been increasing interest in forming new parties more likely to appeal to mainstream voters.

The Patriot Party is organizing in several states to enlist the support of those who voted for Ross Perot in 1992. Many observers believe that Perot's political interest group, United We Stand America, will develop into a political party itself. If it does, it could be a really formidable one, thanks to the millions of people who voted for Perot, and the millions of dollars Perot himself can donate to the cause. Both of these organizations tend to attract relatively conservative voters.

On the more liberal side, the New Party is now struggling to build organizations in at least ten states. Whether it turns out to be liberal, conservative, or something in between, Lowell Weicker, an ex-Republican who is currently an independent governor of Connecticut, predicts that there will be a strong third party "in the field" in 1996.[2]

What can be done to improve the chances of third parties? To give them more of a chance to compete with the major parties for the support, and for the votes, of the public? Jerry Brown suggests that the key is removing some of the unfair advantages the main parties have under the present system.

One of the most important of these advantages has to do with the certification of candidates for office. A place on the ballot is vital to a political candidate. Theoretically, voters can vote for anyone they want to, whether the candidate is on the ballot or not. If their preferred candidate is not on the ballot, they are free to write a name in. As a practical matter, it is almost impossible for a write-in candidate to be elected to national office. And the voting machines that are now being used in most polling places make writing in names more complicated than ever.

As the system works now, Republican and Democrat candidates for national office get on ballots more or less automatically. They are also assured coverage by the news media. This means they will have the opportunity to reach voters, to make their case, and to try to persuade people to vote for them.

Independents and third-party candidates, on the other hand, face daunting procedures in many states before they can even have their names put on a ballot. In Pennsylvania, for example, a party that has at least 15 percent of the state's registered voters is considered "major" and gets on the ballot automatically. Both major parties qualify easily. But for a new party to be classified as major, it would have to register nearly 900,000 voters.[3] Candidates whose parties fail to accomplish that have to collect many thousands of signatures on petitions before they will be put on the ballot. This is often impossible for candidates who are not widely known.

Whether or not a candidate is on the ballot, he or she needs to be heard by the voters to have any chance to win. During his 1992 presidential campaign, Jerry Brown proposed providing "free television and mail under reasonable conditions for every qualified congressional and presidential candidate and party."[4] Just what those "reasonable conditions" might be would be open to debate. But most reformers argue that enough television time would have to be provided for controversial or unknown candidates to explain their unfamiliar views to the public.

Private television stations and networks argue that it would be unfair to force them to give up large amounts of valuable time to political candidates. It would be bad enough if they were ordered to surrender valuable time to Democratic and Republican candidates. It would be totally impractical for them to give up the huge amounts of time needed to provide opportunities to scores of independent candidates. Besides, they say, it would be a waste of time. Few voters would watch.

Another proposal, made by former Democratic activist Ed Garvey among others, is to forbid packaged television campaign commercials altogether. They believe that the highly produced commercials most candidates use are designed to promote an image, to sell a politician like a retail product. This is demeaning to the political process, and misleading to the voters. What's more, these commercials are enormously expensive to produce and air. They contribute more than anything else to the skyrocketing costs of campaigns. The purely informational spots suggested by Brown and Garvey would be much cheaper.

One way to even out the campaign process, and to help voters judge the candidates at the same time, would be to require all candidates to participate in televised debates. Most challengers are eager to debate, but incumbents, who usually have more special-interest money with which to buy TV commercials, and who are already familiar to voters anyway, are often reluctant. Mandatory debates would not only cut down on the incumbents' advantages but they would also reduce all candidates' need for campaign money by giving them free opportunities to air their views. At the same time, presenting all the candidates on one platform would allow them to challenge one another, and give concerned voters the chance to compare them more directly.

OTHER CAMPAIGN REFORMS

Reformers make many proposals designed to cut down the influence of special interests by further limiting the amount that groups and individuals can donate to political campaigns. Jerry Brown, for example, has suggested limiting all political contributions to a maximum of one hundred dollars.

On the face of it, limiting donations seems an obvious way to reducing the unfair effects of big money and the advantage incumbents have in raising it. But as John Fund of the *Wall Street Journal* has pointed out, stricter campaign limits could make it even harder for independent or third-party candidates to challenge major-party incumbents.

Campaign limits are democratic in that they give the advantage to whichever candidate has the *most* contributors rather than to the one with the *wealthiest* contributors. But in practice, the candidate with the most contributors is also the one who is best known, and that is usually the incumbent. Until a candidate has already gotten his or her message out to millions, Fund points out, the candidate can't raise enough money from small contributions to get the message out to millions.[5] As long as campaigns are expensive, the money will have to come from somewhere, and the special interests seem to be the only sources willing to provide the huge sums that candidates require.

The only real alternative seems to be for the government— that is, the taxpayers—to pay for campaigns. This is done, in a small way, for presidential campaigns today. Tax- payers can check a box on their returns contributing three dollars of their taxes to a fund that will be divided among major presidential candidates. Millions of dollars have been distributed in recent elections, although the checkoff was previously limited to only a dollar and only a fraction of taxpayers checked the box.

Jerry Brown and other reformers suggest expanding this method of campaign financing to senate and con- gressional campaigns. Opponents of public financing protest that, in order for the reform to be fair, funds would have to be provided to all legitimate candidates, including independents. That would mean thousands of House and Senate candidates in each election year. With congressional and senatorial campaigns as expensive as they are, this would require an enormous amount of taxpayers' money.

Brown has suggested raising the checkoff to twenty- five dollars to raise the extra money needed, but with relatively few taxpayers willing to contribute even a dol- lar to the presidential campaign fund, it seems unlikely that this scheme would raise enough money to make a real difference. Public financing could be made mandatory, and the money could simply be taken out of the Treasury without a checkoff; but that would mean forcing citizens to support the campaigns of candidates they opposed.

Another campaign reform suggested by Ed Garvey, among others, is limiting the length of campaigns. Some reelection campaigns seem to begin as soon as a candidate takes office. Even the shortest campaigns in the United States go on for many months, in contrast to those in many other democracies, which usually last only a few weeks.

The longer a campaign runs, the more it costs, and the more important large amounts of money become.

———— TOWARD A MORE DIRECT ———— DEMOCRACY

As we have seen, the Founding Fathers chose to have a representative democracy at least partly because a direct democracy was unworkable. The country was just too large, with too many people, for its citizens to gather together. The country is many times larger today, of course, but thanks to modern technology, a form of direct democracy might actually be more feasible now than it was then.

In his independent campaign for president, Ross Perot proposed holding "electronic town meetings." As president, he promised to gather a panel of experts to present the pros and cons of important political proposals on live television. People watching at home could then express their opinions on the issue by using an interactive device hooked up to their television sets.

It wasn't clear how Perot wanted to use such "meetings." Some observers suggested that the sessions could serve as massive opinion polls, which the politicians could take into account in making their decisions. Others proposed that the national town meetings could actually become a form of legal voting—a national referendum in which the people could vote on major pieces of federal legislation right from their homes.

——— BYPASSING THE REPRESENTATIVES ———

The country could actually move a long way toward a more direct democracy even without such high-tech innovations. Greater use could be made of democratic procedures that have been available all along: recalls, initiatives, and referenda. Several states allow for the use of these measures already, and they could easily be used at the federal level, too.

A recall allows unhappy constituents to demand a new election to remove a representative from office before the end of his or her term. In the thirteen states that allow recalls, a new election is scheduled whenever enough voters sign a petition calling for one. The number of signatures needed varies from state to state, but it usually amounts to about one-fourth of the eligible voters.

Initiatives and referenda are ways of bypassing the regular legislative process when elected representatives fail to act. In a referendum, a proposed law or policy is put to a vote by the people. Referenda can be either advisory or binding. When an advisory referendum passes, the legislature has to consider the measure. When a binding referendum passes, it becomes law directly.

An initiative petition allows citizens to actually propose a new law themselves. There are two kinds of initiatives, indirect and direct. In an indirect initiative, when enough people sign petitions asking for a measure, the proposal is put before the legislature. In a direct initiative—or if the legislature refuses to act on a law proposed by a successful indirect initiative—the measure is put onto the ballot as a referendum. Probably the most famous initiative in history was California's Proposition 13 in 1978, by which California voters launched a tax revolt and ordered the state government to cut their property taxes.

There is no question that devices like these are in the spirit of democracy. What's more, they are appealing ideas. Let the people take over. If our representatives fail to act, let's act ourselves.

But some people worry that procedures like these will lead to rash and unwise decisions and harmful results. On the state level, such procedures are usually brought into play when voters are upset about an isolated situation. Citizens start a recall when they are angry with a politician who has cast a controversial vote. Initiatives are launched in response to unusual, and often temporary, conditions. People sometimes tend to vote in the heat of the moment and pass measures they regret later.

Critics worry that voters tend to view intiative and referenda measures in isolation, without much balance or overall perspective. Proposition 13, for example, was seen primarily as way to lower high taxes. In passing it, California voters apparently failed to consider the effects the lower tax receipts would have on the services provided by the state. In the opinion of some observers, Proposition 13 badly damaged California's education system and was at least partly to blame for the economic troubles plaguing California today.

Opponents also argue that such measures are not really as democratic as they seem. Voter turnout in recall, initiative, and referendum elections tends to be unusually light. Most people are not interested enough to go to the polls. As a result, only people who are particularly excited about the matter bother to vote, and an activist minority ends up making a decision for everybody.

So what? a supporter of this more direct form of democracy might respond. People who don't bother to vote are also having their democratic say. They are saying that they have no strong opinion on the issue. They will accept a decision either way. That's a legitimate position. The people who do vote are the ones who have given the most thought to the issue and who know the most about it. Why shouldn't they be the ones to decide?

Opponents protest that the voters are not necessarily the ones who know the most about the issue at all. They are just the ones with the strongest opinion about it, or the ones with the most direct, and often selfish, interests at stake.

Supporters of national referenda argue that they

would allow the voters to bypass the special interests, but John Easterday of Edgewood College in Madison, Wisconsin, believes that they would do just the opposite. He thinks it would be even easier for wealthy special interests to influence referenda on a national scale than it is for them to influence elected representatives.[6]

In Congress there is a process during which the merits of a bill are considered. Studies are done to determine the likely results of passing or not passing the measure. Committee hearings are held to consider changes and alternatives. People and groups on all sides are allowed to lobby. Representatives meet to discuss the issues involved. And finally there is a formal debate during which those on both sides can express their views publicly and respond to each other's arguments.

This is a fairly complicated process. Any special interest wanting to influence it must reach a variety of congresspeople in both houses, each of whom has several other special interests, as as well as their constituents, to consider. For all the complaints about the special interests, it is hard for any single group, no matter how wealthy, to override all these competing influences on over five hundred senators and representatives.

But, Easterday argues, a wealthy and determined special interest might very well control the publicity surrounding a referendum. Easterday argues that public opinion can be fairly easily swayed by a determined public relations campaign. Advertisements, speeches, appearances by celebrities supporting a cause, and television interviews with persuasive advocates can all strongly influence people who don't know very much about an issue.

What's more, propaganda cuts both ways. The ease of swaying public opinion does not always work in favor of an initiative. It can work against it as well. Given the small turnout in special elections, a binding referendum can become an effective veto for any group that can muster enough publicity to get out the vote against a measure.

Supporters of federal initatives and referenda, like James Abourezk an ex-senator from South Dakota, argue that criticisms like these are beside the point. "[I]n one way or another," says Abourezk, "the debate about the voter initiative always comes down to whether politicians trust the American people sufficiently to allow citizens the right to vote directly on the issues."[7] If most politicians distrust initiatives and other forms of direct democracy, many Americans feel a similar distrust of their politicians.

RE-FORMING GOVERNMENT

Chapter 9 dealt with opening up the political process that already exists. In this chapter, we will discuss some proposals often made to change the system itself.

TERM LIMITS

Probably the most frequently suggested reform is setting term limits for federal representatives. As it stands now, congresspeople and senators can return to Washington as often as they can persuade their constituents to reelect them. It is not unusual for congresspeople and senators to spend their entire adult lives in elected office. Claiborne Pell, a Democrat from Rhode Island, has been in the Senate since 1961, for example, and Ted Stevens, a Republican, has served as a senator from Alaska since 1968.

The one exception to this rule is the president. A constitutional amendment limits presidents to two full terms. Many critics of Congress want a similar amendment limiting the terms of congresspeople and senators.

One suggestion is that both should be limited to a maximum of two terms, like the president. Another, that senators be limited to one eight-year term, and congresspeople to three two-year terms. Many other combinations have been suggested. All, however, would ensure that no politician could make a lifetime career out of serving in either body.

The desire for term limits is rooted in a particular idea of the representative's job. Supporters of term limits argue that representatives should not be professional politicians who spend their lives in government. They should be ordinary citizens—businesspeople, doctors, professors, workers—who take some time from their regular lives to represent their neighbors' interests in Washington. Once that time is over, they should return to their ordinary lives and let someone new go to Washington.

The important thing is that they should have ordinary lives to return to. That would keep them in close touch with the people they were sent to Washington to represent, and with the day-to-day needs and concerns of their fellow citizens.

Like many other large cities, Washington, D.C., is surrounded by a highway known as a beltway. Critics complain that even politicians who come to Washington full of fresh ideas and the desire to reform government develop an "inside-the-beltway mentality" once they have been there for a while.

They come to see themselves as members of a powerful elite that runs the country. They become part of a network that includes professional politicians, lobbyists, and wealthy contributors, but excludes the ordinary citizens back home. Term limits would break off that process before an inside-the-beltway mentality could begin to develop.

Supporters of term limits complain that Congress is a kind of incumbent-protection society. They have a point. As we have seen, election laws and practices give terrific advantages to incumbents who run for reelection. (Those laws, of course, were all written by incumbents.) The vast majority of congresspeople and senators use those advantages to return to office again and again. Term limits would turn this process around and ensure a continuing supply of fresh minds, energies, ideas, and ideals into government.

Perhaps most importantly, say the supporters, term limits would end the idea of government as a game in which winning is the only thing that matters. Instead of being obsessed with reelection, politicians would be free to concentrate on solving the nation's problems. What's more, term limits would reduce the influence of the special interests by reducing the need for the money the special interests provide.

There is enormous public support for term limits. As many as 75 percent of people polled favor them.[1] It is as though voters are saying, "I can't help myself. I keep voting for the same people over and over. Please stop me before I do it again."

Despite the widespread public support, however, most incumbent politicians oppose term limits. They obviously have a selfish reason for their opposition: they want to stay in office. But they also have some serious arguments to make.

Enacting term limits would mean forcing many experienced and able legislators out of office. This would be a great loss to the country. Looking back over history, many valuable services have been performed by veteran congresspeople and senators, from conservative Republicans like Robert Taft to liberal Democrats like Lyndon Johnson.

What's more, opponents of term limits insist, it is fundamentally antidemocratic to limit the amount of time an elected representative may serve. Voters, they say, should have a free choice of the person they want to represent them. If the voters of Rhode Island want Senator Pell and the voters of Alaska want Senator Stevens, why shouldn't they have them?

The timidity of elected officials could be bypassed, at least to some extent, by shifting more of the tough decisions on to nonelected officials. This was done in the early 1990s, when the administration of George Bush decided to close a number of military bases around the country.

Closing defense bases tends to be extremely controversial, particularly in the neighborhoods near the bases themselves. Defense bases are economically important to neighboring communities. They usually employ large numbers of local people, and the salaries those people earn, together with the money that military personnel spend in the area, help support all sorts of local businesses. Because communities come to depend on these benefits, they get very upset when bases are scheduled to close. The communities become special interests and exert enormous pressure on political representatives to help keep the bases open. In the past, that pressure was often enough to keep many unnecessary and expensive facilities going—paid for by taxpayers' money.

In order to sidestep that pressure, the administration appointed a special commission to decide which bases to eliminate. None of the members of the Base Closure and Realignment Commission were elected officials, although some had held elected office in the past. Because of this, they were able to act without worrying about the effect their decisions would have on their political future.

Politics was not entirely removed from the process, however. Once the commission made its list of closings, President Bush had to approve it, and then Congress had to vote on the list as a whole. But the vote was up or down— that is, Congress had to vote for all the closings, however controversial some of them might be, or for no closings at all. This removed any possibility of the kind of expensive horse-trading that usually goes into such decisions.

The commission process worked well. People in communities whose bases eventually got the ax were predictably upset, but most observers agreed that the commission had made sensible choices, from both the military and the economic point of view.

Greater reliance on similar commissions could help to undermine the power of special interests and get around the officeholders' obsession with their next election. It could also improve efficiency in government. But would more use of commissions make government any more democratic?

Critics of the commission process argue that it would do just the opposite. Commissions are, after all, designed to remove political pressure from government decision-making, but political pressure—the will of the people—is the essence of democracy.

___ INCREASE THE SIZE OF CONGRESS ___

Many Americans are convinced that the federal government is too big and too far removed from the affairs of ordinary citizens. Ironically, some reformers believe that one answer to this problem may be to *increase* the size of government—or at least the legislative branch of it.

The U.S. Senate has 100 members, and the House of Representatives has 435. That makes 535 federal representatives for 250 million people—or roughly one for every 500,000. This is the poorest ratio of "all the major democracies," says Jerry Climer, of the Congressional Institute.[2] In some districts, the ratio is even worse. One Congressperson in Montana represents 800,000 people.[3]

If the number of senators and congresspersons were doubled, each one would represent only half as many people. That might help make each representative more accessible—and more responsive—to individual constituents.

Several recent presidents have asked for a line-item veto—that is, the power to veto just a part, rather than all, of a bill. They want it primarily as a way to limit government spending by eliminating the pork that lards almost every bill that comes out of Congress.

The way the veto power works today, a president can veto a whole bill or none of it. Because of this, presidents often accept unnecessary pork in order to save the vital elements of the bills containing it. A line-item veto would allow them to slice off the fat while signing the meat into law.

A line-item veto would not have to be limited to spending measures, however. It could be applied to any part of a bill. The governors of some states already have line-item vetoes. Some even have the power to veto individual words. Using this power, they can not only eliminate parts of a measure, they can reverse them. In a bill requiring the government "not to spend state health care funds for abortions," for instance, a governor could veto the word "not." This would turn a "pro-life" provision into a "pro-choice" provision. If the state legislature were closely divided on the abortion issue, it would not be able to override the veto, even though the majority of legislators had passed what they intended to be an anti-abortion measure.

However a presidential line-item veto is designed, it will give more power to presidents than they have today, and encourage presidential leadership. Proponents argue that this would enhance the democratic process. The president, after all, is the only official elected by a vote of all the people, and the people want him or her to lead.

By the same token, a line-item veto would make presidents more clearly accountable for their actions.

They could no longer blame Congress for waste and argue that the legislature forced them to accept pork by attaching it to necessary bills.

Opponents of the line-item veto, however, argue that it is essentially undemocratic to give such power to any single individual, even the president. They argue that presidents are too powerful already. What's more, they say, increasing the veto power could add to government gridlock by making it that much easier for the president to prevent the passage of controversial measures.

___ ADOPT A PARLIAMENTARY SYSTEM ___

The most sweeping reform suggested to solve the gridlock problem is for the United States to adopt a parliamentary system similar to the ones in Canada and England.

A parliament is a legislative body much like our Congress. Elections for seats in parliament are held in legislative districts similar to congressional districts. Whichever party wins the election in a given voting district controls that district's seat in the legislature. A party that wins the majority of seats in the legislature gets to "form a government"—that is, it gets to pick the cabinet ministers and the head of the government, who is called the prime minister.

If no one party wins a clear majority of the seats, parties that control a majority of seats between them can join in a coalition to form a government. The government—whether it is a majority government or a coalition—can remain in power for a set period of time before the prime minister is required to call another election. In England, the maximum time between elections is five years, although the prime minister can call another election at any time during that period.

In many ways, a prime minister is much like a president. He or she runs the executive branch of government and conducts the nation's foreign policy. Together with the cabinet members—who, like the prime minister, are members of parliament—he or she sets the national agenda and proposes legislation to the parliament.

In some respects, however, a prime minister has more effective power than a president because party discipline is enforced in the parliament. In most cases, legislators are expected to vote the way their party decides they should. This means that a prime minister whose party has a majority in the parliament is assured of passing his or her programs without obstruction.

For this reason, the prime minister is more accountable to the voters than an American president because he or she has no one else to blame for government failures. The prime minister cannot blame the parliament, because the prime minister and the parliament act as one.

Unlike American presidents, prime ministers who lose the support of the people can be unseated almost overnight. The members of their own party can dump them at any time simply by choosing a new leader.

If the party itself loses support and members begin to desert the prime minister, the government "falls" and a new election is called. Campaigns tend to be much shorter than in the United States, sometimes taking as little as three weeks.

Political parties become more important under a parliamentary system. There are three main reasons for this: it is the party that chooses the prime minister and forms the government; party discipline is more enforced; and people tend to vote for parties, rather than for individual candidates. As a result, parliamentary parties tend to be more ideological than parties in this country. They exist more as expressions of specific principles and programs, and less as launching pads for individual politicians.

Several advantages of the parliamentary system are

obvious. Gridlock is all but eliminated, and it is relatively easy for the government to get things done. Reforms are easier to accomplish, and even the most sweeping changes in policy are easier to make. Party discipline means less need to compromise and less temptation to lard legislation with costly and wasteful pork.

But perhaps the greatest advantage of all, from a democratic point of view, is that when the majority of people vote for change, they are likely to get it. There is less chance that reforms will be watered down and that the heart will be compromised out of important programs, as it so often is in the U.S. legislative process.

What's more, a parliamentary government is accountable to the voters in a much more immediate way than is our government under the current American system. In the United States today the terms of elected officials are firmly established. If the people decide that they have made a mistake in choosing a president, or if the government fails to accomplish its goals, there is little voters can do until the next scheduled election. Even then, only a certain proportion of elected officials can be replaced at any one time. Under a parliamentary system, the entire elected government can be changed quickly and completely.

On the other hand, the parliamentary system lacks some of the protections built into the U.S. political system. Because the legislative and executive branches are in the hands of the same people, the parliamentary system has fewer checks and balances. The same provisions that make it easier for a parliamentary government to accomplish great changes make it harder for a political minority to protect itself against the power of that government.

Whether or not a parliamentary system would be a good idea for the United States, it is unlikely to be adopted here. As a practical matter, changing to such a system would mean a massive overhaul of the U.S. Constitution, a document that it is very difficult to change. Even to attempt that kind of overhaul would require a national consensus—a general agreement—that the change was necessary. Despite the widespread dissatisfaction with our government, no such agreement is likely any time soon.

Americans are very cautious about changing the Constitution in fundamental ways. Although they complain bitterly about the way the government works, they have an underlying respect for the political system itself, and they are reluctant to tamper with it too drastically.

Most reluctant of all are the politicians who run the government. Under a parliamentary system, individual representatives would be less powerful and less independent than they are now. People who have risen to high office under the current system are not eager to surrender the power and independence they have achieved.

It's impossible to examine our democratic system as we've done in this book without realizing what a messy system it is. It's equally impossible to consider ways of reforming it without realizing that a democracy is bound to be messy, no matter how many reforms are made.

Democracy is not an efficient form of government. It probably cannot be, because it has to protect too many rights and take too many interests into account.

Democracy is often not a very effective form of government, either. As we have seen, democratic procedures make it hard to get things done.

The historian Simon Schama suggests that it may be impossible to have both "a community of free citizens" and a "potent state."[4] If Schama is right, a democracy is bound to be indecisive, wasteful, and relatively weak. That is because a government that has to respect the rights and liberties of its citizens is severely limited in what it can do.

As Thomas Jefferson pointed out more than two centuries ago, "The Government can only do something for the people in proportion as it can do something to the people."[5] The more democratic the government, the less it can do to the people and, however unfortunately, the less it can accomplish.

It may be that a democracy can act swiftly and decisively only in times of great national crisis and immediate danger, as in World War II. Only then do enough private interests come together so that most people are willing to put aside the personal independence a democratic government has no real right to take away.

Centuries of experience have shown that, even at its best, democracy is a difficult, demanding, and dangerous form of government. Yet the democratic ideal is still strong, not just in the United States and other Western nations, but in the world at large.

The United Nations, the one body that represents almost all the countries and peoples of the world, proclaims that democratic ideal in its Declaration of Human Rights. "Everyone has the right to take part in the government of his country, directly or through freely chosen representatives," declares Article 21 of that historic document. "The will of the people shall be the basis of the authority of government."

For all its problems, it seems that democracy really is, as Winston Churchill once said, the worst possible form of government—except for all the others.

SOURCE NOTES

FOREWORD
1. C-SPAN, March 11, 1992.
2. Interviewed by Jan Weller, Wisconsin Public Radio, July 13, 1993.
3. Albert R. Hunt, "How Bad Is It?" *Wall Street Journal*, September 21, 1992.
4. Johannes interview, Wisconsin Public Radio.
5. ABC News poll, announced on *ABC Town Meeting*, ABC-TV, April 10, 1992.
6. C-SPAN, March 16, 1992.

CHAPTER ONE
1. Attributed to the theologian Reinhold Niebuhr by British politician Tony Benn in John Mortimer's *In Character* (London: Penguin, 1983), p. 35.
2. Aristotle, *The Politics*, quoted in *The Democracy Reader*, edited by Diane Ravitch and Abigail Thernstrom (New York: HarperCollins, 1992), p. 9.
3. Ibid.
4. Jefferson's "First Inaugural Address" (1801), reprinted in Paul M. Angle, *By These Words* (New York: Rand McNally, 1954), p. 155.

5. Alexander Hamilton, quoted in Fred Harris, *America's Democracy* (Glenview, Ill.: Scott, Foresman, 1980), p. 41.

CHAPTER TWO

1. James Madison, *Federalist Papers, No. 39,* reprinted in *The Democracy Reader,* edited by Diane Ravitch and Abigail Thernstrom (New York: HarperCollins, 1992), p. 128.

2. Richard N. Current, T. Harry Williams, and Frank Freidel, *American History,* (New York: Knopf, 1975), p. 147.

3. Harris, p. 33.

4. Harris, p. 40.

5. Presidential press conference, excerpted on *The McLaughlin Group,* NBC, July 25, 1993.

6. Benjamin Franklin, "Search at the Constitutional Convention," reprinted in *The Democracy Reader,* p. 111.

7. George Washington, "Farewell Address" (1796), reprinted in Paul. M. Angle, *By These Words* (New York: Rand McNally, 1954), p. 141.

CHAPTER THREE

1. George Washington, "Farewell Address," reprinted in Paul M. Angle, *By These Words* (New York: Rand McNally, 1954), p. 141.

2. Interviewed on C-SPAN, July 28, 1993.

3. Ibid.

4. Ibid.

5. *The McLaughlin Group.*

6. Speaking in front of the U.S. Capitol Building, Washington, D.C., June 24, 1993.

7. Quoted by Howard Phillips, speaking at the National Conservative Student Conference, sponsored by the Young Americans' Foundation, July 26, 1993.

CHAPTER FOUR

1. "Platform in Progress," *We the People,* Campaign Publication, July 1992, p. 4.

2. "Media Perspective on Lobbying Issues," seminar conducted by the Lobbying Institute, American University, June 4, 1993.

3. Albert R. Hunt, "How Bad Is It?" *Wall Street Journal,* September 21, 1992.

4. "Media Perspective."

5. *Donahue* show taping, cablecast over C-SPAN, April 6, 1993.

6. *Federalist Papers,* No. 10, quoted in Fred Harris, *America's Democracy* (Glenview, Ill.: Scott, Foresman, 1980), p. 222.

7. William Greider, *Who Will Tell the People?* (New York: Touchstone, 1993), p. 51.

8. Speaking on C-SPAN, June 14, 1993.

CHAPTER FIVE

1. "Platform in Progress," *We the People,* Campaign Publication, July 1992, p. 4.

2. According to Scott Thomas of the Federal Election Commission, interviewed on C-SPAN, August 17, 1993.

3. *Washington Post,* national weekly edition, May 17–23, 1993.

4. "The Sad, Soiled Face of Politics as Usual," *Los Angeles Times,* July 27, 1993.

5. Judi Hasson and Jessica Less, "Dinner Renews Fund-raising Criticism," *USA Today,* April 28, 1992.

6. "Bundles of Bucks for Campaign '92," *U.S. News & World Report,* May 4, 1992.

7. *Washington Post,* national weekly edition, May 17–23, 1993.

8. Judi Hasson and Jessica Less, "Dinner Renews Fund-raising Criticism," *USA Today,* April 28, 1992.

9. Interviewed on *Special Assignment,* CNN, July 19, 1993.

10. "Tsongas's Money Ceiling," *Wall Street Journal,* March 23, 1992.

11. Ibid.

12. "Interviewed on "Washington Under the Influence," *On the Issues,* PBS, June 6, 1993.

13. Presidential Candidate Debate, Richmond, Va., Oct. 15, 1992.

CHAPTER SIX

1. Speaking on *This Week,* ABC-TV, August 1, 1993.

2. *Conversation with Howard Baker, Jeane Kirkpatrick, and Pierre Salinger,* C-SPAN, July 4, 1993.

3. Speaking on *The McLaughlin Group,* NBC, August 1, 1993.

4. *Nightline,* ABC-TV, July 30, 1993.

5. Ibid.

6. Richard Wolf, "Too big, too busy, and too beholden," *USA Today,* April 28, 1992.

7. "Bush, Congress Have Dug Heels In," *USA Today,* April 28, 1992.

8. *Talk of the Nation,* National Public Radio, June 16, 1993.

CHAPTER SEVEN

1. Edmund Burke's speech on his election to Parliament, in *The Democracy Reader,* edited by Diane Ravitch and Abigail Thernstrom (New York: HarperCollins, 1992), p. 51.

2. Speaking on *The Capital Gang,* CNN, August 13, 1993.

3. Quoted by Senator Mitch McConnell, *American Profile,* C-SPAN, November 26, 1992.

4. Speaking on *Meet the Press,* NBC-TV, July 25, 1993.

5. William Greider, *Who Will Tell the People?* (New York: Touchstone, 1992), p. 271.

6. Interviewed on C-SPAN, July 21, 1992.

CHAPTER EIGHT

1. Speaking on C-SPAN, March 20, 1992.

2. Tsongas and ex-senator Warren Rudman were briefing the editorial boards of the *Arizona Gazette* and the *Phoenix Telegraph,* July 8, 1993.

3. Cablecast of hearing, C-SPAN, March 18, 1992.

CHAPTER NINE

1. "Speech to the Constitutional Convention," quoted in *The Democracy Reader,* edited by Diane Ravitch and Abigail Thernstrom (New York: HarperCollins, 1992), p. 111.

2. Appearing on *Crossfire,* CNN, November 5, 1992.

3. Gerald F. Seid, "Political Stirrings," *Wall Street Journal,* August 4, 1993.

4. "Platform in Progress," *We the People,* July 1992, p. 4.

5. Ibid.

6. Speaking on Wisconsin Public Radio, March 18, 1992.

7. Fred R. Harris, *America's Democracy: The Ideal and the Reality* (Glenview, Ill.: Scott, Foresman, 1980), p. 310.

CHAPTER TEN

1. John H. Fund and James K. Coyne, "End of Term for Governing Class," from *Cleaning House* (Washington, D.C.: Regnery Gateway, 1992), *Wall Street Journal,* October 9, 1992.

2. "Call for Bigger House Finds Increased Support," *USA Today,* March 30, 1992.

3. Ibid.

4. Simon Schama, *Citizens: A Chronicle of the French Revolution* (New York: Knopf, 1989), p. 16.

5. Quoted in William F. Buckley Jr., *Rumbles Left and Right* (New York: Putnam, 1963), p. 126.

BIBLIOGRAPHY

Birnbaum, Jeffrey H. *Showdown at Gucci Gulch.* New York: Vintage, 1987.

Boyte, Harry C. *Commonwealth: A Return to Citizen Politics.* New York: Free Press, 1989.

Etizioni, Amitai. *Capital Corruption, the New Attack on American Democracy.* San Diego: Harcourt Brace Jovanovich, 1984.

Fund, John H., and James K. Coyne. *Cleaning House.* Washington, D.C.: Regnery Gateway, 1992.

Greider, William. *Who Will Tell the People?* New York: Touchstone, 1992.

Harris, Fred. *America's Democracy: The Ideal and the Reality.* Glenview, Ill.: Scott, Foresman, 1980.

Magleby, David B., and Candice J. Nelson. *The Money Chase: Congressional Campaign Finance Reform.* Washington, D.C.: Brookings Institute, 1990.

Mansbridge, Jane J. *Beyond Adversary Democracy.* New York: Basic Books, 1980.

Margolis, Michael. *Viable Democracy.* New York: St. Martin's, 1979.

Peters, Charles. *How Washington Really Works.* Reading, Mass.: Addison-Wesley, 1980.

Vogel, David. *Fluctuating Fortunes: The Political Power of Business in America.* New York: Basic Books, 1989.

*　*　*

The books listed on the previous page deal with various aspects of the modern American political system. The two anthologies listed below provide a valuable context for considering that system. The first offers selections from a wide range of key documents and speeches that throw light on the development of democracy in the United States. The second offers similar selections drawn from the history of the entire world.

Angle, Paul M., ed. *By These Words.* New York: Rand McNally, 1954.

Ravitch, Diane, and Abigail Thernstrom. *The Democracy Reader.* New York: HarperCollins, 1992.

INDEX